BROAD STREET
TO
POPLAR

A PHOTOGRAPHIC
JOURNEY

By J.E. Connor

CONTENTS

Published by

CONNOR & BUTLER

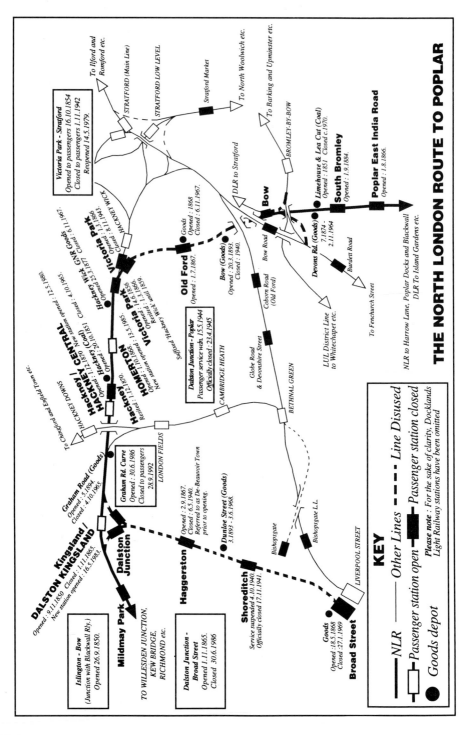

THE NORTH LONDON ROUTE TO POPLAR

Victoria Park - Stratford
Opened to passengers 16.10.1854
Closed to passengers 1.11.1942
Reopened 14.5.1979.

STRATFORD (Main Line)

STRATFORD LOW LEVEL

To Ilford and Romford etc.

Stratford Market

To North Woolwich etc.

To Barking and Upminster etc.

BROMLEY-BY-BOW

DLR to Stratford

Limehouse & Lea Cut (Coal)
Opened : 1851 Closed c.1970.

South Bromley
Opened : 1.9.1884.

Poplar East India Road
Opened : 1.8.1866.

Hackney Wick GNR Goods : Closed : 6.11.1967.

Victoria Park
Opened 25.3.1877
Closed : 8.11.1943

HACKNEY WICK

Old Ford (Goods)
Opened : 1868
Closed : 6.11.1967.

Bow (Goods)
Opened : 20.3.1893.
Closed : 1940.

Bow

Devons Rd. (Goods)
7.1874 -
2.11.1964

Bow Road

Burdett Road

Coborn Road
(Old Ford)

To Fenchurch Street

LUL District Line
to Whitechapel etc.

HACKNEY / CENTRAL
HACKNEY : 1.12.1870 New station opened : 12.5.1980.
Opened : Hackney : 20.10.1851 Closed : 4.10.1965.
Opened 5.9.1894.

HOMERTON
Resited : 1.12.1868 ; 13.5.1985.

Victoria Park
Opened : 10.1863 ; 14.6.1856
New station opened 14.6.1986
Resited : 1.1.1859
Suffixed 'Hackney Wick' until 1859.

Saffixed 'Hackney'

Dalston Junction - Poplar
Passenger service wdn. 15.5.1944
Officially closed : 23.4.1945

CAMBRIDGE HEATH

Globe Road
& Devonshire Street

BETHNAL GREEN

Graham Road (Goods)
Opened : 9.11.1850
Closed : 4.10.1965.

Graham Rd. Curve
Opened : 30.6.1986
Closed to passengers
28.9.1992

LONDON FIELDS

To Chingford and Enfield Town etc.

HACKNEY DOWNS

**Dalston Kingsland /
DALSTON KINGSLAND**
Opened : 9.11.1850 Closed : 1.11.1865.
New station opened : 16.5.1983.

Dalston Junction

Mildmay Park

Islington - Bow
(Junction with Blackwall Rly.)
Opened 26.9.1850.

TO WILLESDEN JUNCTION,
KEW BRIDGE,
RICHMOND etc.

Haggerston
Opened : 2.9.1867.
Closed : 6.5.1940.
Referred to as De-Beauvoir Town
prior to opening.

Dunloe Street (Goods)
3.1.1893 - 3.6.1968.

Shoreditch
Service suspended 4.10.1940.
Officially closed 17.11.1941.

**Dalston Junction -
Broad Street**
Opened 1.11.1865.
Closed 30.6.1986.

Bishopsgate

Bishopsgate L.L.

LIVERPOOL STREET

Goods
Opened 18.5.1868
Closed 27.1.1969

Broad Street

NLR to Harrow Lane, Poplar Docks and Blackwall
DLR To Island Gardens etc.

KEY

—— NLR   —— Other Lines   ---- *Line Disused*

▭ Passenger station open   ▬ Passenger station closed

● Goods depot

Please note : For the sake of clarity, Docklands
Light Railway stations have been omitted

2

PREFACE

When I was a child, one of the places where my parents took me shopping was Chrisp Street Market. To get there we would walk from our flat in Stepney Green through the bombed-out streets to Commercial Road, and catch a 567 trolleybus. I remember the bridge over the railway at Poplar, because, if I was lucky, we'd hear a rush of steam, and Dad would hold me up so I could look over the wall. Of course it was always a goods train, but that never seemed particularly unusual to a four or five year old who just wanted to see the engine!

As I grew older my interest developed, and I began to take my first photographs. One day I was with a friend from south London wandering around the back streets of Bow trying to find a way into Devons Road shed. By this time the place had been completely dieselised, but we'd read that the sole surviving B12 4-6-0 was stored there, and we wanted to get some pictures. We didn't have a Shed Directory with us, and had no luck in gaining access. Because I came from the East End my friend naturally thought I knew the area's railways, but unfortunately at that time I was more familiar with the main line termini, and had little idea as to the location of the entrance to Devons Road. We climbed up onto the roof of a pram shed in a block of council flats to see if we could find a way to the depot, and there, just the other side of the wall, was a very overgrown island platform. We hadn't found the shed, but we had found the last vestiges of South Bromley station.

My friend seemed unimpressed, but to me there was something about the place which exuded a kind of magic. I was fascinated.

I tried to learn as much as I could about the line, but found nothing in the book shops. Admittedly there had recently been an article on the North London in *The Railway Magazine*, but although this was obviously very learned, it said very little about the stations themselves, and therefore was unable to provide me with the information I wanted. There was nothing for it but to go out with the camera, and record what I could before their remains disappeared completely.

Armed with a tatty, incomplete vintage A-Z, I started seeking out the old Poplar line stations, and taking a few photographs of each. Sometimes I was well rewarded, such as with the fine street level building at Old Ford, or else I'd be well and truly disappointed, as I was at Homerton where very little survived.

About 1969 I started work on a magazine article about the line, but it seemed to be getting a bit lengthy, so I abandoned it before completion. I stuffed it into an old envelope where it remained until the 1970s. I then rediscovered it, and with encouragement from my wife finally had it published as the book 'All Stations To Poplar'. This seems to have sold well, so when I first became involved in publishing, it seemed a good idea to bring it up to date, and re-release it.

We only printed a small number of these, and they sold out very quickly. Since then we have been asked on numerous occasions to make it available again, but I was never happy with the idea, as I felt that it should include much more information. Therefore, in response to all those who have asked me about 'The Poplar Book', here it is in very much modified form. I hope it proves to be of interest to all, who like me, find the London railway scene of yesteryear a source of endless fascination.

J.E. Connor
Colchester
January 1995

INTRODUCTION

On 26th August 1846, the Royal Assent was given authorising the construction of a eight mile railway running from north London through to the East End. It was to originate at a junction with the London & Birmingham line near Camden Town, then proceed by way of Islington, Hackney and Bow. It was known by the rather unwieldy title of The East & West India Docks & Birmingham Junction Railway, and was intended chiefly as a freight link between the towns of the Midlands and the docks at Blackwall.

Construction proved to be slow, largely due to financial problems, but further hampered when some of the works collapsed at the western end. Therefore it wasn't until 26th September 1850 that the first trains ran, and then only east of Islington. Although intended for goods traffic, the initial service was for passengers, and operated from Islington to the London & Blackwall's City terminus at Fenchurch Street. This was made possible by the construction of a junction between the new enterprise and the Blackwall Extension Railway near Bow Common.

The E&WID&BJR was an immediate success, and carried a total of 97,000 passengers during its first month.

Train services were extended westward to Camden Town on 7th December 1850, and Hampstead Road on 9th July 1851.

On 20th October 1851, the line between Bow and the docks was finally brought into use, although this was originally for coal traffic only. The first trains were operated by the Northumberland & Durham Coal Company, who used their own locomotives and wagons, but this proved impractical, and the workings were taken over by the Railway in 1859. The line was opened to general freight from 1st January 1852, and to passengers on 1st August 1866.

The Company's title proved a bit of a problem. It was very wordy, and although technically correct in that it linked the London & Birmingham with the East and West India Docks, it could scarcely be regarded as describing the area it served. A writer in the *Illustrated London News* of 15th November 1851 referred to it as *'The Camden Town Railway'*, and this seems to be how the line was commonly known at the time. After a while, the authorities agreed that the official name was too cumbersome, and an Act was passed enabling it to be changed to the much more appropriate *'North London Railway'* from 1st January 1853.

Traffic continued to grow, both passenger and freight, and it eventually became obvious that the NLR was fast outgrowing the limited facilities available at Fenchurch Street. Therefore an Act was obtained in 1861 which authorised the construction of a extension linking Dalston with a new City terminus opposite Old Broad Street. This was opened on 1st November 1865, and referred to at the time as 'The Happy Afterthought'.

A very esoteric NLR curiosity brought about by this was that although trains travelling from Broad Street towards Bow would quite naturally be described as 'down', as soon as they reached Dalston they would be called 'up'. This odd throw-back to the days when North London services went *up* from Dalston to Fenchurch Street stayed with the Poplar line until the end of its days, and must have caused confusion to staff who were unfamiliar with it.

Throughout its existence, the North London Railway had strong associations with the London & North Western, and even in its early days had sixteen of its twenty-four directors appointed by the LNW. It nevertheless remained nominally independent until 1922, although its operation had been taken over by the larger company some years previously on 1st February 1909.

The LNWR had also been closely involved in the opening of the line to Broad Street, and paid a considerable amount towards its construction. In return for this they had the use of half the terminus, and served it with their own trains. In 1911, a scheme was approved to electrify the North Western suburban system, and five years later, on 1st October 1916, passenger workings to Richmond and Kew Bridge were taken over by electric units.

Despite this affinity to a larger company, the North London always had a very individual character, and nowhere was this more apparent than in the appearance of its stations. From the 1860s until 1875, the Company employed the services of Edwin Henry Horne as architect, and the buildings he designed had a style all of their own. Historians have described them in many ways including 'Italianate', 'Moorish' and 'Lombardic', but whatever the correct architectural description, they were certainly distinctive. The cavernous structures at street level were clearly built to impress, with windows and doors topped with semi-circular arches, and the railway's name emblasoned in a cement rendered frieze just below the roofline. Unfortunately the majority of these have now been demolished, although examples can still be seen at Hackney and Camden Road, together with a similar, if less ornate building at Acton Central on the former North & South Western Junction line.

Like many other inner-suburban railways, the fortunes of the Poplar branch took a serious knock with the coming of improved road transport, but perhaps this was inevitable. The rolling stock used was never of the highest quality, even in the early days, and could hardly have been comfortable to travel in. According to an interview with Mr. George Bolland Newton, the NLR General Manager in *The Railway Magazine* for September 1898, the original carriages had bodies built of papier mache, which must have been flimsy, and certainly would not conform to modern safety measures! For many years, coaches used on the Poplar service were gaslit four-wheelers marshalled in close-coupled formations, with a brake van at either end.

On 21st March 1927, George Lansbury, the local MP made an emotive plea in the House of Commons for better travelling conditions on the railways of the East End, and he made particular mention of the North London Line. He referred to the coaching stock as *"coming out of the ark"*, and above the sneers and laughs of his fellow politicians he said: *",,,it's really not a matter to joke about. For two or three years I have not had to ride on the railway, but lately I have done so, and I am shocked each night as I go down, and each morning as I come up at the condition of overcrowding, which the wives and daughters and sisters of the working people have to endure."*

No wonder the East Enders preferred to travel by 'bus or tram.

With the Grouping of 1923, the North London Line became part of the London Midland & Scottish Railway, then on nationalisation in 1948 its ownership was transferred to the Midland Region of British Railways.

The North London was badly affected during the Second World War, and the Poplar branch suffered in particular. The East End was mercilessly pounded throughout the Blitz, and of course, the railways and docks were regarded by the Luftwaffe as military targets. As a result, the passenger trains were withdrawn from 15th May 1944, and the stations closed. For a while the booking offices remained open to issue tickets for replacement 'buses, but this arrangement ceased on 23rd April 1945.

For over a century, the Poplar branch was worked by steam, with various types of locomotive employed. From the 1860s onwards, the majority of passenger trains were hauled by a succession of sturdy and reliable 4-4-0Ts, which were developed by the Company's engineer, William Adams, from a Robert Stephenson & Co. design of 1855. Basically the NLR-built engines fell into two categories, the earlier type were fitted with inside cylinders, whilst the later variety had them outside. Having said that there were numerous detail differences within the classes, and the subject deserves a book on its own.

When Adams left Bow to join the Great Eastern at Stratford, he was succeeded by Mr. John C. Park, who created his niche in railway history by designing a robust 0-6-0T for North London freight services, whose mighty hauling power ensured their survival well into BR days. Both these and the 4-4-0 passenger tanks were responsible for most of the work on the Poplar line until the advent of the LMS. Mr. Park began his career at the Great Southern & Western Railway works at Inchicore in Dublin. From here he moved to Doncaster, where he was employed under Patrick Stirling as Chief Draughtsman for the Great Northern. He came to Bow as Locomotive Superintendant in 1873, and stayed for twenty years. On retirement, he was replaced by Henry Pryce, who had been with the Company since 1878. Pryce had previously been in charge of the Signalling and Telegraph departments, and on gaining promotion also assumed responsibility for engines and rolling stock. He remained in charge until the end

5

of 1908, when he agreed to retire prior to the LNWR taking control.

North London engines were originally painted in mid-green, set off with white/black/white lining and polished brasswork, but after 1883 this was replaced by a more sombre black, lined out in pale blue-grey and red. The subject of liveries is very complex and again merits a study in its own right.

After 1924, the LMS introduced their standard 0-6-0T goods engines to the line, which had been designed at Derby under the direction of Henry Fowler, and later became known as 'Jinties'. These were used for both freight and passenger, and were fitted with destination board brackets to conform with North London practice. In 1925 they tried out five ex-North Staffordshire Railway 2-4-0Ts, but these proved to be under-powered, and after a short period of being shedded at Bow, were soon disposed of.

Unfortunately, space does not permit anything approaching an in-depth study of the line's motive power, but hopefully sometime in the future another writer will set to the task, and produce that much needed volume on North London locomotive matters.

To those of us who knew the Poplar line in its postwar freight-only period, the developments since 1979 still seem a little unreal. Back in the Sixties, there was an occasional snippet in one of the local newspapers suggesting that it should reopen to passengers, but no-one could have predicted the changes which would eventually happen. Having said that, it didn't require a twentieth century Nostradamus to predict the end of poor old Broad Street, but the coming of the Docklands Light Railway, with its driverless trains speeding between Bow and Poplar would have seemed the stuff of fantasy. A few years earlier, passenger trains began operating again between Dalston and Stratford, and now there is the possibility of the East London Line taking over the trackbed of the old City extension. It seems that so much of what was once dead has got a future after all, and that the route has a place in the London of the 21st Century.

As the years progress, there is less and less to be seen of the old features of the NLR line to Poplar, and unfortunately very few photographs appear to have been taken. The purpose of this little book is to gather together some of the more interesting pictures, and present them with a brief history of the line. In some cases, photographs of less than perfect quality have had to be used, but many are unique, and are possibly the only views of these subjects in existence. We travel from Broad Street to Dalston Junction, and then through Victoria Park and Bow to Poplar. I hope the reader finds the journey fascinating, and enjoys a glimpse of an East End which is now only a memory.

NLR 4-4-0T No.8 stands at Devons Road shed on 22nd August 1901. Some years earlier, on the night of 28th January 1882, it was involved in a serious collision near Old Ford, resulting in the loss of five lives. Damage to the engine was comparatively light, and it was soon repaired.
H.L. Hopwood / LCGB Ken Nunn Collection

THE ROUTE DESCRIBED

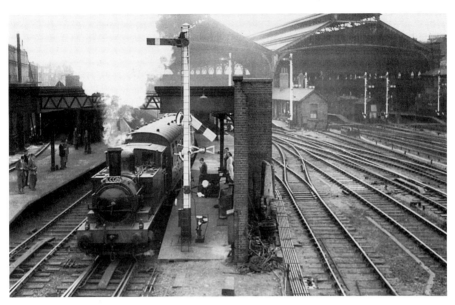

The Locomotive Club of Great Britain's *'Poplar & Edgware'* special train leaves Broad Street on 5th May 1956, behind ex-NLR Park 0-6-0T No.58859. The tour travelled first to Poplar, then round to Millwall Junction, where locomotives were changed, and *'Jinty'* 0-6-0T No.47484 took over. It then headed via East Ham and Stratford to Canonbury, where Gresley N2 0-6-2T No. 69506 backed on to work over the Alexandra Palace and Edgware branches. The N2 eventually brought the train back to Canonbury, where 58898 was waiting to take over for the short hop back to Broad Street.

Lens of Sutton

BROAD STREET

To look at the site of Broad Street station today, it is impossible to imagine the fine building which once stood there. The Broadgate office development of the 1980s, has completely eradicated all signs of the terminus, and even the most discerning eye will see nothing to indicate where it once stood.

For the lover of Victoriana, Broad Street in its heyday was a wonderful place. It was a vast, impressive edifice, and when opened in 1865, the North London Railway were justifiably proud of it.

The main building, which faced onto the north side of Liverpool Street, opposite the end of Old Broad Street, was constructed of white Suffolk bricks, embellished with Portland stone, terracotta, and Peterhead granite. It was constructed in 1864 on the site of the erstwhile burial ground which adjoined the notorious Bedlam lunatic asylum, and boasted a central clock tower, which rose to a height of around seventy-five feet. Inside, at street level, there were originally two wooden booking offices; one on the east side for the North London, and one on the west for the LNWR. From these, staircases ascended to the platforms, which were located on viaduct above.

When first opened, Broad Street had seven platforms, which were covered by a glazed overall roof. This consisted of two 95' spans, and had a total length of over 457'. It was supported on either side by the station's outer walls, and in the centre by a row of ornamental cast iron columns. The roof was designed by the LNWR chief engineer, William Baker, and was constructed in a manner which would not preclude alterations to the platform layout, should these prove necessary in the future. The platforms on the east side were designated solely for the North London, whilst those on the west played host to 'Outer Circle' workings, and services operated to and from suburban stations on the LNWR.

The terminus, together with the new line from Dalston cost £1,200,000 to build, and was opened to the public on 1st November 1865, following a banquet for the Lord Mayor, and various City dignitaries which was held the previous day. It was an immediate success, and in a short time, the North London's traffic more than doubled.

Trains for Chalk Farm departed every quarter of an hour, as did services to Bow and Fenchurch Street. In December 1865, the time allowed for the almost circular trip between these two City termini was thirty-three minutes, which included stops at Shoreditch, Dalston Junction, Hackney, Victoria Park, Bow and Stepney. After 1st August 1866, these workings were diverted south of Bow to serve the newly opened line to Poplar. The journey time for down trains was twenty-six minutes, but up trains did it in four minutes less.

In addition to these services, there were also trains which connected Broad Street with Kew, and a little later, Richmond and Watford.

On 18th May 1868, the London & North Western Railway opened a large goods depot immediately west of Broad Street station, with street level facilities connected to the yard above by hydraulic wagon lifts. Prior to this, the LNWR's only City freight terminal was at Haydon Square, which was situated on a short branch off the London & Blackwall line near Fenchurch Street.

As built, the line between Dalston Junction and Broad Street comprised of only three tracks, one down, and two up, but with increasing traffic, both passenger and goods, this arrangement soon needed to be altered, and therefore a fourth track was added to the west of the formation between 1874 and 1876. At around this time, the layout on the west side of the terminus was changed slightly, and provided with scissors crossovers at the stop blocks end to improve locomotive run-round facilities. Additional traffic was generated from 18th January 1875, when a service was introduced between Broad Street and suburban stations on the Great Northern Railway, which they reached by way of the Canonbury - Finsbury Park spur, then newly opened to passengers. With so many trains now using the terminus, modifications to layout again became essential, and in 1891, an eighth platform was provided on the east side.

A little earlier, on 4th September 1890, the original booking offices were closed, and replaced by a new structure located on the concourse. Following this, the two internal staircases were removed, and the station's street level frontage converted to accommodate a row of eight shops. To maintain access, a pair of stairways were constructed at the front of the building, and connected to the platforms by means of covered iron footbridges. These were constructed above the cab road, and led to two arcades adjoining the concourse, each of which was provided with shops. The erection of these new bridges required the demolition of a sizeable chunk of ornate *porte-cochere* which previously graced the facade, and although they no doubt improved passenger flow, they also spoilt the building's appearance.

Broad Street, was in its prime in the early years of this century, with around 80,000 passengers a day passing through. In 1902, the writer A.J. Chisholm described the station thus: *"It is a substantially built structure. The long straight platforms are paved with stone. The rails run over lengthy engine pits, which extend from one end of the station to the other, as regards platforms 1, 2, 3, 4, and up to the cross-over roads at platforms 5,6,7,8. The roof being high, is of noble dimensions. There is plenty of glass overhead, which is cleaned at regular intervals. Altogether the building may truly be described as a stately pile. It is to be hoped that electric light will soon find its way into this commodious station, as the present lighting arrangements are far from satisfactory."*

With business booming, it became apparent that the station needed yet more expansion, and

Above : The concourse at Broad Street looking east in post-Second World War days, showing the wooden offices which were replaced in 1957 by new brick-built structures.

Author's Collection

Below : The external staircase on the east side of Broad Street station was an attractive architectural feature. It was carefully dismantled in 1985, during the early stages of the building's demolition, and put into store for possible erection elsewhere.

J.E. Connor

therefore in 1911, work began on the construction of a ninth platform. As there was no more room available beneath the overall roof, it had to be located outside the western retaining wall, necessitating the strengthening of supporting girders, and the rearrangement of tracks in the adjoining goods yard.

The Central London Railway extended their line eastwards from Bank to Liverpool Street on 28th July 1912, and constructed a booking hall for their new terminus beneath Broad Street's forecourt. This opened a little under three months later on 10th October, and was provided with a pair of escalators. Better interchange facilities between the new line and the North London came on 23rd February 1913, when two lifts were installed giving direct access from the Broad Street concourse. These were accompanied by a small booking office on the upper landing for the issue of Tube tickets, and through bookings to and from the Underground were introduced. Later that year, a Portland stone facade was completed around Broad Street's forecourt which incorporated entrances to both the NLR and the Central London. For its day it was stark and modern, and certainly did little to harmonise with the style of the 1865 terminus. In his book 'London's Historic Railway Stations', the late Sir John Betjeman referred to it as *"a silly entrance facade...without any regard to the architecture behind"*, and maybe he was right.

In its heyday, the station had all the refinements associated with a main line terminus, with a dining room, first and second class refreshment rooms, and a bookstall. However, the majority of its passenger traffic was purely of a suburban nature, although on 1st February 1910, the LNWR introduced an express train for businessmen, known as 'The City to City'. The up train originated at Wolverhampton, and called only at Birmingham and Coventry on its journey to London, whilst the return trip in the evening was similar, but made an additional stop at Willesden Junction. To encourage patronage, the company employed a typist, who travelled on the train, and typed letters for passengers during the journey, but the enterprise sadly failed with the onset of World War One. The up train succumbed from 22nd February 1915, having survived its counterpart travelling in the opposite direction by a little over seven months.

The War also brought disruption of a different kind to Broad Street. On 8th September 1915, a bomb dropped from a Zeppelin landed in Sun Street Passage, which was situated immediately to the east of the station, and caused the destruction of a thousand panes of glass in the overall roof. In the same raid, two 'buses were hit nearby, causing a number of deaths, and some horses stabled in the goods yard were injured.

On 1st October 1916, despite the shortage of men and materials brought about by the war, the route linking Broad Street with Richmond and Kew Bridge was electrified by the LNWR, but the two tracks on the east side of the viaduct, between the terminus and Dalston Junction remained unaffected.

With the end of the War in 1918, things gradually returned to normal, although 'The City to City' was never restored. In February 1921, a memorial was unveiled on the concourse at Broad Street to commemorate the sixty four members of North London staff who died in the War.

On 1st January 1923, the North London, which had been operated by the LNWR since 1909, became part of the huge London, Midland & Scottish Railway, and Broad Street found itself as one of the London termini of the LMS.

By this time, tram and omnibus competition was beginning to erode some of the station's traditional traffic, although for a time at least, it continued to be busy. In an attempt to relieve congestion at Fenchurch Street, the infant LMS introduced a through service between Southend and Broad Street, therefore generating extra business. With this in operation, more people were using the east side of the station, and new canopies were added at the northern end of platforms 1, 2 and 3 to provide extra shelter.

The Second World War had devastating effects on the line in general, and the Luftwaffe made numerous hits along the route. Bombing of the approach tracks at the beginning of October 1940 put Broad Street out of action for a number of days, and marked the start of a decline from which parts of the former NLR would never recover. The East End suffered particularly during the air-raids, and having sustained a great deal of damage, the line between Dalston and Poplar finally lost its passenger trains from 15th May 1944.

When peace returned in 1945, the North London Line and the area it served well and truly showed the scars of the relentless bombing it had suffered, although Broad Street itself had not suffered too badly. Nevertheless, with its East End services gone, and the Richmond electrics not exactly operating to capacity, the future was beginning to look bleak. For all this, the line continued to operate, and the concourse at Broad Street even received a half-hearted attempt at modernisation. This came in the middle of 1957, when the old wooden offices, erected in 1890, were swept away, and replaced by two new brick built structures of typically plain post-war appearance. These comprised booking and enquiry facilities, together with a Station Master's office, and toilets. Whilst this work was being carried out, a number of boxes of used NLR tickets were discovered, dating back to the end of the last century. After a period of some years, these eventually surfaced at the late lamented Museum of British Transport in Clapham, and many were sold off to private collectors at *'Surplus Relics Sales'* for a few old pence each.

With traffic very much on the decline, it came as no surprise when the remaining section of the North London system was proposed for closure in Dr. Beeching's report, *'The Reshaping of British Railways'*, which was published on 27th March 1963. Notices were posted at stations along the line, announcing a proposed date for the end of the year, but after a great deal of pressure from local councils, it won a reprieve. However, for a while things still seemed very uncertain, and it wasn't until July 1965 that the Broad Street - Richmond route was finally struck off the closure list.

In the meantime, the poor old City terminus continued to deteriorate. The overall roof was shortened between 1967 and 1968, after a section at the northern end became unsafe, and platforms 1, 2, 3 and 9 were taken out of use on 3rd November 1969. Their tracks were lifted shortly afterwards. The former platform 4 became No.1, and the others were renumbered accordingly.

By the 1970s the concourse appeared empty and ghostlike, and the new brick offices, put up in 1957, stood with the NLR war memorial amidst a sea of desolation. The erstwhile refreshment room, locked and forlorn since 1963, lay with its mirrors and decorative stained glass very much the worse for their years of neglect. Up until the mid-1980s, it was still possible to find Festival of Britain stickers on two of its grime encrusted windows, inviting thirsty travellers to enjoy a cup of tea: The slogan underneath read *"Britain's national drink in Festival Year"*. It seemed all very sad and poignant. In front of the former refreshment room doorways were a pair of tatty rubber mats, which continued to bear the initials of the LMS, albeit just vaguely discernable beneath the accumulation of grime. Nearby, on the concourse, in a special glass case, once stood a model of NLR 4-4-0T No.60, which had been built by apprentices at Bow Locomotive Works in 1888. Originally this had worked on steam, but latterly an electric motor was fitted, enabling the wheels to turn when a pre-decimal penny was dropped into the slot. It was removed in 1970, and eventually taken to the National Railway Museum, York, where it can still be found.

More seeds of destruction were sown when the services onto the former Great Northern were axed. These had been solely operated by multiple units since May 1969, but the last train, which ran on Saturday 6th November 1976 was actually loco-hauled, although not surprisingly, this was an enthusiasts' special.

With its services drastically reduced, the huge, crumbling structure began to appear even more desolate than before. The ticket office was closed in the early 1970s, and replaced by a self-service machine. The station, already seemingly deserted now had even less visible staff, although an occasional railman showed up to collect tickets at the barrier. The trackbed which once served the platforms on the east side became a tangle of weeds, with wild buddleia bushes sprouting their bright purple sprays above lesser, more humdrum foliage. There was still a signal box however. The former No.2 box, which adjoined the country end of the western wall continued to be staffed, although train movements were far from complex. Box No.1 had stood between the tracks which once served the original platforms 2 and 3, but this closed on 3rd November 1969, and after demolition, its site was quickly engulfed in undergrowth.

By the late 1970s, the concourse shops had long-since ceased trading, and the station bookstall was just a fading memory, but once a year, the remaining staff would do their best to cheer the place up by erecting an illuminated Christmas tree. This would stand near the former booking office, and look pathetically incongruous, surrounded as it was by echoing emptiness and decay.

It was pretty obvious that Broad Street had no future, but as to how and when it would meet its end still remained to be seen. The adjoining goods depot closed on 27th January 1969, and was demolished in the early '70s, leaving a gaping space alongside the viaduct, which soon found use as a car park.

In 1976, British Rail announced their desire to amalgamate Broad Street with the adjoining Liverpool Street terminus of the former Great Eastern, and to use surplus land for commercial development. There followed a public enquiry into the scheme, and planning permission was eventually granted in 1979.

Land in the City has always been valuable, and even when the station complex was being designed back in the 1860s, the planners were careful to fit all they could into a fairly tight area of just two and a half acres. With the boom in office development which was taking place in the late 1970s and early 1980s, the redevelopment scheme clearly offered lucrative prospects.

The idea was to totally rebuild Liverpool Street, and divert the North London trains into there by means of a new spur near Hackney. This would diverge from NLR metals, close to a former goods yard at Graham Road, and join the Liverpool Street line near London Fields.

A service of diesel units started operating between Camden Road and North Woolwich on 14th May 1979. These ran in addition to the Broad Street electrics, and used the route through Kingsland and Victoria Park to Stratford Low Level. Electrification of this route would enable the Richmond trains to operate to North Woolwich, and therefore divert them away from Broad Street. Obviously there was an outcry, but British Rail insisted that by changing at Highbury onto the Northern City or Victoria Line tubes, passengers could still reach Central London with the minimum of fuss.

Withdrawal notices for Broad Street went up in 1981, stating that during the interim period before Liverpool Street was completed, it would be replaced by a temporary station 600 yards

The concourse at Broad Street in 1980. Behind the war memorial can be seen the former parcels office, which by this time had been leased to a firm of builders.

J.E. Connor

to the north in Worship Street. This received the go-ahead early in 1983, with the proviso that replacement 'buses would be available to carry passengers into the City. However, within twelve months the plan was dropped, and nothing came of it.

A full electric service to North Woolwich was eventually introduced on 13th May 1985, and Broad Street was left with just a few peak hour workings to and from Watford. The stage was now set for the kill.

Closure of the line to Broad Street would of course also entail the abandonment of Dalston Junction, which although scarcely a shadow of its former self, was still in regular use. However since 16th May 1983, a new station called Dalston Kingsland had been served by the North Woolwich trains, and therefore the loss was deemed acceptable.

In accordance with their proposal, British Rail began construction of the single track spur near Graham Road, which would enable the meagre Watford workings still using Broad Street to run into Liverpool Street, and the fate of Broad Street was sealed.

There was a degree of protest against its forthcoming demise, and a 'Save Broad Street' campaign was launched, but all to little avail. The developers were eager to get started, and British Rail were just as eager to assist. From Monday 1st July 1985, the main building was closed, and a temporary entrance was provided in Sun Street Passage, near the site of the 1915 air-raid incident. A scaffolding stairway led passengers from the doorway up to track level, where a wooden hut sufficed as booking office, waiting room, and staff facilities. From here, access was made to the remaining platform.

In the month prior to this, the preliminary stages of demolition included the careful removal of the war memorial, which was taken down piece by piece, and removed by road to Richmond, where it was eventually re-erected. There was nothing particularly careful about the rest of the demolition however, except that is for the dismantling of an ornate stairway which stood on the eastern side of the station, and was referred to by John Betjeman as being of 'Lombardic' style. This was again removed from the site by road, and put into storage for possible use elsewhere.

Demolition of the main building and remains of the overall roof was swift, and thorough. For some time, one of the lift shafts which once led to the Central London Railway, still stood amidst the mountain of rubble, and was clearly visible above the roadside hoardings, a few green and white tiles clinging to one of its walls.

In seemingly no time the faded grandeur that was Broad Street had gone. A few peak hour trains still rumbled in and out, but these used a temporary wooden extension which had been erected at the northern end of Platform 4, and little of the fine terminus remained.

Closure was proposed for May 1986, but delays in the completion of the Graham Road spur ruled this out. The end eventually came a few weeks later on the evening of 27th June, when the final train, the 18.37 departure for Watford Junction, formed of unit 313 008 departed to the traditional sounds of exploding detonators.

Poor old Broad Street, a long time dying, was now officially dead.

BROAD STREET - SHOREDITCH
Even in its final days, a journey from the old terminus was still one which was full of railway interest.

From the window of a departing train, passengers could look down from the viaduct and glimpse Liverpool Street station, which was originally opened by the Great Eastern in 1874 and subsequently enlarged. Until comparatively recently it had changed little over the years, but it has now been extensively and tastefully rebuilt. This work was partly financed by the sale of the Broad Street site, and was completed in December 1991.

The ground once occupied by the old North London terminus has been completely engulfed by the Broadgate development, and the stretch of viaduct south of Worship Street has met a similar fate.

The approach tracks to Broad Street were once very busy, but latterly they became rationalised and overgrown. Just outside the station, to the east of the line stood New Inn Yard signal box, which was operational from 1875 until 11th April 1969. This was quickly followed by another box, known as Skinner Street. A cabin with this name existed from the time that the

13

line first opened, but the one which survived into the twentieth century was sited further north. It was constructed around 1875/6, and remained in use until 15th February 1970.

Between these two boxes, the line passed over Great Eastern Street, and, on the east side, passengers could catch sight of the original Eastern Counties Shoreditch terminus, which was rebuilt into Bishopsgate goods depot in 1881, and destroyed by fire in December 1964. After closure, the ruined buildings were demolished, and the site eventually used as a car park.

The NLR viaduct continued northwards, and the line was carried on a bridge above Old Street, where the first station out of the terminus was sited.

SHOREDITCH

Shoreditch was the earliest intermediate station on the City Extension, and opened along with the line in November 1865. Its entrance was situated at the junction of Old Street and Kingsland Road, and its main building was a typical example of the Company's architecture. It consisted of two storeys, with a booking office on the ground floor, and internal stairways which provided access to the platforms. There were a pair of double doorways which led from Kingsland Road, and an additional door beside the bridge in Old Street. All of these, together with the adjoining windows were topped by segmental arches of red brick and Portland stone, whilst the structure itself appears to have been built largely from yellow stocks. The south-eastern corner of the upper floor had three pairs of arched windows, which were adorned in a similar fashion, and displayed a liberal amount of 'Moorish' detailing.

There were two platforms, both of which served the lines on the east side of the viaduct, although one was an island, and could be used by up trains from the Willesden direction if required. When the No.2 down line was added in 1874, some minor rebuilding seems to have taken place, but the general layout remained unaltered, and no extra platforms were constructed. The island accommodated a group of three wooden buildings which housed from south to north, a gents' lavatory, a ladies room, a 1st Class waiting room, the stairway to the booking

NLR 4-4-0T No.68 stands at Shoreditch with a train of LNWR stock in the first decade of the twentieth century.

Lens of Sutton

Above : Shoreditch station looking north in the 1930s, with a *'Jinty'* hauled passenger train standing at the up platform.

Photographer unknown : Author's collection.

Below : Shoreditch station, looking in the opposite direction, again in the 1930s. The buildings on the island platform remained virtually intact until 1965, despite having been out of use since 1940.

David Hanson Collection

office, with porters room attached, and a general waiting room. There was also a two storey brick built structure at the northern end, which latterly incorporated a gentlemen's toilet, replacing the facilities at the south end, which closed in LMS days. It is possible that this was rebuilt from the lower portion of the original signal box, which was replaced at the time of the widening. The three wooden buildings were joined together by an awning which covered about three-quarters of the station's length, and this was matched by a similar canopy on the opposite side. The up platform originally measured 370 ft., but was lengthened by a further 66 ft. around 1875. Accomodation comprised a general waiting room, a station inspector's office, a ladies' room, and the stairs to the street.

The new signal box erected around the time of the widening, stood about 40ft. from the north end of the island platform. At some time prior to 1894, another box was constructed on the west side of the viaduct, just beyond where the line crossed Old Street. This was designated Shoreditch No.2, whilst the other became 'No.1'.

Widening of Old Street in 1927, and Kingsland Road two years later, necessitated the reconstruction of the street level building, and this was completed in 1928. The replacement consisted of three storeys instead of the original two, and much of it was intended for use as commercial premises. Whilst this work was in progress, the contractors, Messrs. Walter Scott & Middleton, had to remove the platform buildings which stood on the Old Street bridge, and replace them like for like when the job was finished.

Because of war damage to the surrounding trackwork and viaduct, trains ceased to call at Shoreditch from 4th October 1940, although the booking office remained open until 17th November the following year to issue tickets valid on replacement 'buses, and to deal with parcels. After this period however, the Company thought otherwise, and the station was permanently closed. .

Shoreditch station weathered the ravages of war comparatively well, and the only damage directly attributable to enemy action was its broken windows. This aside, the buildings on the island platform remained more or less intact for an incredible period of twenty-four years, although by this time they had become rather derelict, and parts of their awnings had been removed.

Unfortunately, the fact that the place had survived for so long was not appreciated by everybody, and every so often, commuters would write letters to the press grumbling about the 'eyesore' which they had to endure on their journeys to and from the office. In response to these and other trivial complaints, British Rail announced the introduction of a 'Clean-Up The North London Line Scheme' in 1965, which not only resulted in the partial demolition of Shoreditch, but also led to the wanton destruction of many fine and interesting buildings elsewhere along the route. Virtually all the stations still in use had their original structures torn down, and replaced. Meagre, if functional little brick booking offices were constructed at street level, whilst the platforms received dreadful metal and glass waiting shelters, which soon provided hours of enjoyment for vandals.

Shoreditch however somehow lingered on, and it wasn't until the early 1970s that the central building which housed the stairway, and the former men's lavatory were finally removed from the island platform.

Latterly the station presented a sorry sight, with its platforms lying broken and overgrown. At the City end of the down side, a decapitated rusty lamp-post still poked bravely through the weeds, whilst the track level part of the main building was leased out as a workshop. Down below however, the old booking hall remained much as it had since closure, and its interior could be clearly seen from the street. The tile work was still intact, and was typical of the period when the structure was rebuilt. There was a small boarded-up window, still displaying the words 'TICKETS - BOOK HERE', and this was centred between a pair of rectangular spaces, which until the mid-1960s still bore traces of pre-war posters. During the 1980s, the old folding barriers which separated the station from the pavement were taken down, and replaced by heavy metal gates, making it impossible to look inside. Above the former entrance there are positioned two sets of windows, and these are adorned by a cement surround which exhibits tendencies towards the style popularly known as 'Art-Deco'. This includes a symbolic winged wheel motif, and is topped by three carved brick panels which carry the legend '19 - LMS - 28'.

When the scheme to extend the East London Line to Dalston was in its initial stages, it was intended that Shoreditch would be rebuilt and brought back into use. However, platforms positioned on such a tight curve were felt to fall below current safety standards, and the idea was dropped in favour of a completely new station, a little further north, to be called Hoxton.

Immediately beyond Shoreditch, the line was carried over Kingsland Road on an impressive girder bridge, which for its last few years of use was painted in an unpleasant shade of yellow ochre.

DUNLOE STREET GOODS DEPOT, SHOREDITCH

On the up side, north of this bridge, was situated Shoreditch, Dunloe Street goods depot, which was opened by the LNWR in the Spring of 1893. This was located between Cremer Street and Pearson Street, and had facilities at both rail and road level. Coal was dealt with by means of chutes, which led down to storage bins and bagging machines, whilst the section handling general goods traffic was equipped with a hydraulic wagon lift. Hydraulics were also used for shunting purposes, and capstans were placed at strategic positions throughout the yard. The depot closed on 3rd June 1968, and was eventually dismantled. During the final years of the line into Broad Street, little could be seen of it, other than a large empty space, and a solitary cast iron plate on the parapet which marked the site of a former capstan.

Before work could start on building the depot, a wooden signal box, which stood on stilts to the east of the viaduct had to be removed. This was replaced by a new thirty-five lever cabin on the opposite side of the line, which took the name of Dunloe Street, and remained in use until 2nd December 1976. The derelict structure survived a little longer, but was eventually demolished in April 1985.

Beyond here, the line crossed the Regents Canal, and skirted the district of De-Beauvoir Town, built to the west of Kingsland Road in the early 1840s, and named after its developer, Richard Benyon de-Beauvoir.

HAGGERSTON

Close by was situated Haggerston station, which was opened on 2nd September 1867. From the original drawings, it appears that the Company intended to name it De-Beauvoir Town, but changed their minds before completion.

Its entrance took the form of a double-storey building, constructed largely of yellow stocks, which stood on the south side of Lee Street. In here could be found the booking office, where in later days rain would drip through a hole in the ceiling, and make life very uncomfortable for the clerk on duty. By the late 1930s, the station was comparatively little used, and this was reflected by the number of unissued pre-grouping tickets still gathering dust in the racks.

At track level, the general layout was similar to Shoreditch, with platforms serving the original three roads only, and nothing facing the line which was added in 1874. There were two signal boxes, of which 'No.1' was situated at the north end of the island, whilst 'No. 2' was built out from the viaduct, at the station's south end.

With the coming of the Second World War, Haggerston became an obvious candidate for closure, and trains ceased to call from 6th May 1940. A few months later, in October, the main building was hit by German bombs and part of its frontage badly damaged. At an unspecified date, 'No. 1' signal box was also bombed, and subsequently demolished.

The wooden platform buildings lingered on some time after closure, but had gone by the early 1960s. Eventually there was very little left of the platforms themselves, and what did remain lay submerged beneath a sea of foliage.

The proposed East London Line Extension has a station planned for Haggerston, which will be on the site of the original. However, as hardly anything now remains of its predecessor, it will be a totally new structure.

Immediately beyond Haggerston, the line began to descend, first on a gradient of 1 in 112, then 1 in 60, until by the next station, Dalston Junction, it was in cutting.

Two views of Haggerston station, both looking towards Broad Street in the late 1930s.
Above : The up side. *Below :* The island platform.
The station was latterly little used, and closed as a wartime economy on 6th May 1940. During the October of that year, the main building was damaged in an air-raid, and was eventually demolished. Of all the stations on the North London which survived into the twentieth century, Haggerston seems to have been one of the least photographed, and therefore these pictures are extremely rare.

David Hanson Collection

DALSTON JUNCTION

Dalston Junction opened along with the City Extension on 1st November 1865, and once boasted a total of six platform faces. Numbers 1 to 4 were on the west side, serving Chalk Farm, Richmond and Great Northern line trains, whilst numbers 5 and 6 curved sharply to the east towards Poplar. Its main entrance stood on the south side of Dalston Lane, just east of the junction with Kingsland Road, and was a single storey structure built mainly of yellow stock bricks. Its architectural styling was instantly recognisable as 'NLR', but was less imposing than others on the line, which seems strange considering its importance. A further booking hall, known as 'The East Office', is believed to have been located in Roseberry Place, and connected to the Broad Street end of the platforms by a covered footbridge, although information on this is very sketchy. Track level buildings were constructed mainly of wood, and these provided all the usual facilities, including, at one time, a refreshment room.

On 29th October 1899, the station featured in a particularly repugnant murder case, when a three and a half year old illegitimate boy was killed by his mother. The woman's name was Louise Massett, described as *"36 year old French governess"*, and her son was named Manfred. For some time he had been placed in the care of another family, but one day his mother collected him on the pretence of sending him away to school. She led him to Dalston Junction, bought him a bun in the buffet, then proceeded to the Ladies Room on Platform 3, where he was knocked unconscious with a brick and finally strangled. She then dumped his body behind one of the toilets and callously went off for a weekend with her current young lover in Brighton. Police had no difficulty tracking her down, and she was soon arrested. At her trial, she was found guilty, and subsequently sent to the gallows.

In common with other stations on the North London, the years following the Second World War brought a period of decline to Dalston Junction, and the place began to look decidedly shabby. It nevertheless remained fairly intact for some time, despite being partially disused. Although the awnings on platforms 1, 2 and 3 had been shortened by 1957, no real attempt at demolition took place until the early '60s, when the buildings on platforms 4, 5 and 6 were removed, together with the footbridge at the Broad Street end. At the same time, an imposing and prominent section of glazed roofing, which existed above the foot of the stairs on platforms 4 and 5, was also taken down. The work was more or less completed by 1964, although rubble remained lying around for a little longer.

The station now looked very bare, with buildings on the west side only, and a new, spartan footbridge leading from the booking office. Further rationalisation came in the early part of 1967, when the remaining platform buildings were swept away and replaced by small glass and metal waiting shelters. The street level was next to go, finally succumbing in January 1970. Dalston Junction was now looking very sad indeed.

The tracks which once led to Poplar were lifted around 1966, and the area levelled. A minor curiosity which survived until about this time was a large British Railways maroon nameboard, which clung to the wall at the northern end of platform 6. Considering this had been out of use since 1944, it seems strange that BR saw fit to put it up in the first place!

A wooden signal box, complete with attractive valencing survived at the Broad Street end of platforms 2 and 3 until 1985, and represented the sole surviving item of architectural interest on the station. Just to the south of here were once a group of 86ft 6in signal posts, specially constructed in 1886 to be clearly visible above the Forest Road bridge, but these had long gone, having been demolished in 1956.

By the time Dalston Junction closed at the end of June 1986, it had become a very desolate place, with empty windswept platforms, and just two tracks in operation. The remainder of the station was overgrown and derelict, with a scrapyard occupying much of the land on the east side.

After closure, it didn't take long for nature to reclaim the place, and within a year, a jungle of bushes proliferated over the entire site. Some of the black-on-white corporate image British Rail nameboards, put up in the late 1960s still remained in situ, poking out of the weeds, but being made of plastic, they were easy to break, and soon vandalised.

Above : The frontage of Dalston Junction in the early years of this century,
with a horse tram for Shoreditch trundling by.

Commercial postcard : Author's Coillection.

Below : The Poplar line platforms at Dalston Junction, looking towards Broad Street c.1950.

Author's Collection.

If the proposed East London Line Extension comes into being, it is intended to open a new station on the site, which will possibly incorporate parts of the *'Lombardic'* stairway, carefully removed from Broad Street in the Summer of 1985, and subsequently stored.

DALSTON JUNCTION - HACKNEY

Beyond Dalston, the Poplar line turned east, and joined the original Islington to Bow route near Dalston Lane. On the north side of this curve stood Kingsland depot, opened for coal traffic by the NLR on 20th October 1851, and subsequently enlarged by the LNW to handle general merchandise from 1st November 1870. It served the district for well over a century, and remained in use until 7th August 1972.

West of the former junction stand the two platforms of Dalston Kingsland, opened on the site of the long-abandoned Kingsland station on 16th May 1983. Kingsland was one of the earliest stations on what later became the NLR, and opened on 9th November 1850. It was rendered redundant with the opening of the route to Broad Street, and therefore closed from 1st November 1865. All track level relics disappeared many years ago, but the main building, on the west side of Kingsland High Street miraculously survived as commercial premises until January 1982. Its demolition proved necessary for the construction of the present station, and nothing of the original now survives. Dalston Kingsland cost £650,000 to construct, of which £166,000 was provided by grants from the Greater London Council, and the Department of Transport's Environmental Urban Programme. Although trains began to call on 16th May, the official opening ceremony had to wait until the following day, when the Chairman of the GLC Transport Committee, Mr. David Wetzel officiated, and a plethora of publicity material, ranging from leaflets to balloons was handed out to announce the event.

Between the converging lines from Broad Street and Kingsland stood Dalston East Junction signal box, which has now vanished without trace.

The former street level building at Kingsland in 1965.
Closed in 1865, it was converted into commercial premises, and lasted until 1982, when it was demolished to provide a site for the present Dalston Kingsland station.

J.E. Connor

The line continues eastward, and the Graham Road Curve diverges to the south at Navarino Road Junction. This was opened on 30th June 1986 to provide access from the North London to Liverpool Street, and closed to passengers from 28th September 1992. It was used by a few trains in peak hours, but now only sees the odd empty stock working. This spur partly occupies land once used by the former Graham Road goods depot, opened by the Great Eastern in May 1894, and closed on 4th October 1965.

The North London remains on an easterly course, and passes beneath the Great Eastern route to Chingford and Enfield on its approach to Hackney station.

THE ORIGINAL HACKNEY STATION

The first premises at Hackney were opened with the line on 26th September 1850, and featured a substantial building butting up to the viaduct on the east side of Mare Street. Adjoining this was a goods and coal depot, which was brought into use on 20th October 1851.

The Illustrated London News' of 15th November 1851 contained an account of a journey between Fenchurch Street and Camden Town, which includes the following description: *"We have now arrived at the Hackney Station: on the right, from the midst of roofs of houses and the thickly planted trees in the churchyard, rises the picturesque tower of the old church; and to the right, the pyramidal tower of the new church. Looking leftward, we were somewhat puzzled at the appearance of several long ditches, or rather trenches, filled with running water, nearly covered with what we took to be weeds; but, upon inquiry, we found that this was one of the artificial streams for the continual growth of watercresses for the London market. Annexed is a singular species of cultivation, which affords a living to a great number of poor men, women and children. The square building on the right side is the Hackney Railway Station; here the train halted for a few seconds, and then moved on towards Kingsland, which is in a deep cutting passing under the Kingsland-road."*

Thirteen years later, Hackney station again found its way into the newspapers, but this time in a far less pleasant manner.

THE FIRST RAILWAY MURDER

On the evening of Saturday 9th July 1864, a pair of young clerks employed at Robart's Bank in the City made their way to the booking office, and bought a couple of First Class tickets to Islington.

After waiting on the platform for a short while, they saw the 21.50 train from Fenchurch Street approaching, and when it stopped, they made their way to a First Class compartment. As one of them sat down, he noticed the seat was wet and sticky, and peering at the upholstery through the gloom of the dimly lit carriage, he found it to be covered with blood. He and his companion yelled for the guard who came rushing along the platform to see what had happened. As he shone his handlamp into the compartment he saw that blood appeared to be splattered everywhere, and that a travelling bag, silver-knobbed walking stick, and man's hat were lying on the floor between the seats. There was no sign of any victim however, so as the train was already running four minutes late, he locked the carriage door, and gave the "Right Away".

In the meantime, an empty stock working was trundling along between Victoria Park and Bow stations, when its driver saw a dark huddled shape lying across the six-foot way in front of him. He immediately applied his brakes, and brought the train to a stand with its engine just a few feet from the obstruction. Both the driver and guard leapt down on to the ballast, and found the 'object' to be a badly beaten, unconscious man. They called for help, and with the assistance of some local people and a policeman, the man was carried to the nearby *'Mitford Castle'* public house.

Amongst the victim's possessions was a letter, which identified him as William Briggs, Chief Clerk at Robart's Bank, which by some extremely odd coincidence, happened to be the same place of work as the two young men who discovered the blood soaked compartment at Hackney. He was taken to his home at 5, Clapton Square, but died later from extensive head injuries.

The North London had just witnessed the first railway murder.

The story has been told and retold many times elsewhere, and space precludes the inclusion of too much detail here. However, suffice to say that after some good, old fashioned detective work on behalf of Inspector Tanner of Scotland Yard, a warrant was issued for the arrest of a German emigre named Franz Muller. He was eventually captured, after a dramatic trans-Atlantic chase, and brought to trial. He was found guilty and was publicly executed on 14th November 1864. He protested his innocence to the very end, although was reported to have confessed to a Lutheran Minister just before his death.

To lay the fears of nervous travellers, some railway companies responded to the murder by placing small windows at the tops of compartment partitions, which although cutting down to an extent on privacy, at least made people feel safe. These were used on many lines, including some overseas, and became known internationally as *'Muller's Lights'*.

Street level view of the second station at Hackney, some time in the early 1900s
Commercial postcard : Michael Cox Collection

THE SECOND STATION AT HACKNEY

The original Hackney station was closed and replaced by a new one on the opposite side of Mare Street on 1st December 1870, after which it was demolished.

Its successor comprised two platforms and boasted a double storey street level building designed by the Company's architect E. H. Horne. From 1st December 1885, covered footways were opened linking the west end of the platforms with the Great Eastern station at Hackney Downs, and these led to a booking office, which was staffed by the GER, but issued both companies tickets. This interchange remained in use for most of the station's existence, although it was closed as a wartime economy in 1917, and didn't reopen until 1923.

When passenger services east of Dalston Junction were withdrawn on 15th May 1944, Hackney station was of course closed, although in common with other stations on the line, the booking office remained open until 23rd April the following year to issue tickets which were valid on the replacement 'bus.

Little visible damage appears to have occurred during the Second World War, but dereliction

NLR 4-4-0T No.27, departs from Hackney with the 5.42pm Bow - Broad Street train
on 24th April 1912.

LCGB Ken Nunn Collection

became apparent after closure. A writer in the periodical *'Trains Illustrated'* for March 1954 describes a journey on a cross-London freight and states *"We rumbled through Hackney, where a little more of the station roof seems to have collapsed since I last saw it..."* Demolition of the platform buildings commenced around this time, and by 1964, very little remained standing.

The main building survived, begrimed and gaunt alongside the bridge in Mare Street, as did a few fragments on the City-bound platform, but other than this there was little of any substance. Humps beside the tracks indicated the site of the platforms, and it was just possible to pick out glimpses of broken surfacing beneath the growth of weeds. Above the former entrance, a pair of cement plaques, one above the other, once displayed the legend *'North London Railway - Hackney Station'*, but these had been rendered over, apparently during the *'Phoney War'* period of 1939, when numerous signs showing names were obliterated in an attempt to confuse the enemy should they invade.

Following the introduction of the Camden Road - North Woolwich passenger service in May 1979, work was put in hand constructing a new station on the site, and within a short while the premises began to take shape. Early publicity showed the name as 'Hackney', but in a BR timetable, an LT fares list and on signs around the site it appeared as 'Mare Street'. However, before the job was completed the authorities had another change of mind, and by the time it opened on 12th May 1980, it carried the title 'Hackney Central'.

To those of us who only knew the main building as a sad, blackened remnant of a long-closed station, it came as a culture shock to see it in its original yellow brick, and it seemed even stranger when a nameboard appeared on the frontage. This little touch was to prove very temporary however, as BR decided not to use the old edifice after all, and to construct a ticket office on the Woolwich-bound platform with direct access from the street.

The two new platforms are connected by a footbridge, and there are small brick shelters on either side. When trains first started calling the station was still unfinished, and even the name-

Above : Hackney station, looking towards Poplar in the late 1930s. The signal box is just visible in the mist beyond the platform canopy on the right.

Below : Hackney station, looking in the opposite direction, presumably on the same occasion. Unfortunately both views are rather un-sharp, but that do provide a valuable record of a little-photographed station.

Both : David Hanson Collection

Above : Ex-NLR 4-4-0T No. 2852 at Hackney station on 16th January 1927
with a Poplar - Broad Street train.

H. C. Casserley

Below : An identified LMS *'Jinty'* 0-6-0T passes Hackney with a coal train around the same date.
The board on the right advises North London passengers to change for destinations on the
former Great Eastern, whilst the GER line itself can just be seen on the bridge in the distance.

Lens of Sutton

boards had not gone up. This was soon remedied although both Hackney Central, and Hackney Wick, a new station east of Victoria Park, had to wait until Wednesday 11th June 1980 for the then Chairman of British Rail, Sir Peter Parker, and Mr. Horace Cutler, Leader of the GLC to come along and declare them officially open.

Today, the old street level building still stands, and is used, as it has been for many years, by a firm of greengrocers. An attractive porch which once graced the frontage was replaced in the early months of 1980 by a glass canopy, but other than this the structure is intact, and is one of only three examples of NLR station architecture to survive. Up above, a short section of retaining wall still stands at the east end of the Richmond-bound platform, but everything else, not that there was much anyway, disappeared with the construction of Hackney Central.

Before the present station was built, it was still possible to see the course of the old covered way leading to the former GER premises at Hackney Downs, together with an intact stairway and the little interchange booking office. The stairs have now disappeared however, and although there are still traces of the old office, the remains are nowhere near as obvious as they once were.

The long gone Hackney signal box stood to the south of the viaduct, immediately east of Mare Street, and beyond its site, on the opposite side of the line can be seen traces of the coal depot, which finally closed on 4th October 1965.

The cavernous street level building at Homerton in the early 1900s. A painted sign on the bridge over Barnabas Road advertises Third Class tickets to Poplar for 2d single or 3d return. The building was demolished by the early 1960s, and only a fragment of the frontage now survives. The present station entrance is on the opposite side of the line.

Colin Mansell Collection

HOMERTON

The next station is at Homerton, and this was first opened on 1st October 1868. Its entrance in Barnabas Road originally took the shape of a huge single storey building, taller in fact than the adjoining railway bridge, and from the few photographs which exist, one can imagine what a cold, cavernous place it must have been inside. At track level, the buildings were of brick construction, protected from the weather by canopies which stretched about two-thirds of the platforms' length.

During the latter part of the nineteenth century, Homerton must have been a very busy place, and at peak times the booking clerks found it very difficult to cope with the crowds. By 1898, the demand for special Workmen's Tickets had become extremely heavy on this line, and the Sweetmeat Automatic Delivery Company were commissioned to supply dispensing machines at certain stations. One each of these was provided at Hackney, Victoria Park, Old Ford and Bow, but such was the need at Homerton that two had to be installed.

For all this, the station later suffered the same period of decline, and few people missed it when it closed with the rest of the line in 1944.

After closure, the great yawning structure became dangerous, and although it survived well into the 1950s, it was eventually demolished. The meagre remains presented an air of total desolation, and it wasn't long before ragwort covered the broken platforms where workmen once jostled for their penny train to town.

Following the re-introduction of passenger services over the line, work commenced on a new station for Homerton, and this opened on 13th May 1985. It occupies the site of its predecessor, and utilises the original passenger subway, but the platforms are shorter than before. The entrance is still in Barnabas Road, but now consists of a small brick building to the south of the line. The rebuilding was approved by the GLC Transport Committee in January 1984, and cost £440,000 to complete, with the necessary finance provided by the Hackney Partnership Scheme.

The lower section of original frontage remains standing, and the more observant can still see a stone step, which once led into the booking office, worn down by countless pairs of hobnailed boots as men trudged through the station, to and from their places of work.

Beneath the west end of the platforms runs a very low arch, which was constructed as a cattle creep, and provides a souvenir of the early days of the line when cows grazed in nearby meadows. The 1851 article in *'The Illustrated London News'* previously referred to describes the scene thus: *"Passing onward, through verdant fields, we came to the retired village of Homerton..."* This may seem very unreal now, but it must be remembered that until the coming of railways, places such as Homerton and Hackney were indeed villages, separated from the city by tracts of open countryside.

Homerton, looking towards Broad Street on 25th February 1950.

Author's Collection

HOMERTON - VICTORIA PARK

Beyond Homerton, the line continues eastward, and the site of the former Hackney Wick goods and coal depot can be seen on the north side. This was opened by the Great Northern Railway on 25th March 1877, and closed on 6th November 1967. Until the mid-1980s, a large, dark blue Eastern Region nameboard remained in-situ above its former entrance in Kenworthy Road, but this has now been removed.

Here the route begins to curve to the south, and Victoria Park come into view.

The park itself was laid out by the architect James Pennethorne on over two-hundred acres of land formerly known as Bishop Bonner's Fields, and was opened to the public in 1845.

VICTORIA PARK, HACKNEY WICK

In 1856, the North London Railway constructed a station on the north side of Wick Road, and named it Victoria Park. This was specially brought into use on 29th May of that year in connection with celebrations to commemorate the end of the Crimean War, but the official public opening did not come until 14th June. It was initially shown in timetables as 'Victoria Park, Hackney Wick', but the suffix was dropped after 1859.

It consisted of two short platforms, originally without any shelter, but waiting rooms and awnings were later constructed. In time however, these premises proved inadequate, and were therefore superseded by a larger station, sited further east.

THE SECOND VICTORIA PARK STATION

The new establishment opened on 1st March 1866, and was a direct replacement for the original which closed from the same date.

It consisted of four platforms, two of which were on the Poplar line, whilst the others served the Great Eastern tracks leading to Stratford.

This branch was opened by the Eastern Counties Railway on 15th August 1854, but for the first month or so it had been very lightly used. However, things began to look up after the NLR introduced passenger trains over it on 16th October, and regular freights began running on 1st January 1855. The early passenger workings originated at Hampstead Road, and comprised around two coaches which would be coupled at the end of a train bound for Fenchurch Street. On arrival at Victoria Park Junction, these would be detached, then taken through to Stratford Bridge on the North Woolwich line where they would terminate. This was all comparatively easy, but the return working never proved so practical. Various methods were tried, but none seemed particularly successful. Sometimes the carriages from Stratford were attached at the front of the main train, or sometimes at the back, but either way it involved some complex shunt moves. With the opening of the first Victoria Park station, the attaching and detaching of stock was carried out whilst the train was at the platform, but it still proved time consuming and potentially dangerous, so was eventually discontinued. From 1st July 1855, the NL introduced a limited number of trains between Hampstead Road and Tilbury, by way of Victoria Park and Forest Gate Junction, but these were presumably unsuccessful, and withdrawn after just a few months. All through workings ceased on 1st November 1866, when the GER began operating a local service which shuttled up and down between Stratford Bridge and Victoria Park. For some reason these trains were referred to by the nickname of 'Stratford Jack'.

The new Victoria Park station had an entrance which faced onto Cadogan Terrace, and although owned, and staffed by the NLR, also issued tickets for the Great Eastern. The main building overlooked one of the park gates, and comprised three storeys, with a booking hall on the ground floor. Architecturally it differed from the other structures on the line, and was rather less ornate in its detailing.

Royalty paid a visit on 6th May 1882, when Queen Victoria boarded a special train for Chingford, where she performed a ceremony dedicating Epping Forest to the public. The engine used was 0-4-4T No.189, which had been specially painted blue for the event by the GER. Obviously the company officials must have been pleased with the result, as from then until the advent of the First World War, blue became the standard Great Eastern loco livery.

From 24th February 1891, a footbridge was brought into use linking three of the platforms at Victoria Park, but not that serving the up Stratford line, which by then was virtually abandoned. Access to this had always been by means of a boarded crossing, which was scarcely the safest way of joining a train. It was never well used, and work on its demolition was completed on 15th August 1895.

The station itself continued to prosper however, and patronage was so good that a second entrance became necessary. Local residents suggested Gainsborough Square as its location, but because this would prove too costly, the Company chose Riseholme Street instead. This became known as the *'Hackney Wick Entrance'*, or as it was shown on tickets 'Victoria Park No.2'.

The Cadogan Square frontage of Victoria Park station in the early 1900s
Charles Martin Series postcard No. 861 : Author's Collection

Throughout its existence, the Poplar services continued much as they always had, with a train running every fifteen minutes, but the Stratford line workings were subject to change. Although the GER took over their operation in 1866, North London engines worked them on alternative years until 1874. From 1st October 1895, these trains began running to and from Canning Town, where they normally terminated in a bay. At first these ran half-hourly, but the frequency was reduced to hourly, presumably as a wartime economy from 1st January 1917. Unfortunately the service never recovered, and having suffered further cuts in 1921, ceased to operate on Sundays from 7th October 1923.

Declining fortunes also started to affect the North London side, and from the 11th July 1920, it was announced that the Riseholme Street entrance would only open during the peaks. From here on it's the same old story. *'Victoria Park No.2'* closed from the 29th January 1940, and the Stratford line trains withdrawn from 1st November 1942.

On Thursday 14th January 1943, a meeting was held at the station to discuss its total closure. This was attended by various officials from both the LMS and the LNER, together with the station master from Hackney, who was also responsible for Victoria Park. Various reasons for closure were given, ranging from the general dilapidated condition of the buildings, through to the decline in passenger receipts, but it was doubtlessly the latter which proved most damning. It was stated that during the year 1929 there had been 470,119 passenger journeys, which had

Above : Victoria Park station as it appeared c1910.
The platform in the foreground served the Great Eastern Stratford trains, whilst the NLR Poplar line is on the right. A fourth platform, which was situated beside the up Great Eastern track was little used, and demolished in 1895.

D. Brennand Collection

Below : The Poplar line platforms at Victoria Park, viewed from the Broad Street end on 22nd February 1950. By this time a certain amount of demolition had already taken place, including the erstwhile footbridge.

Author's Collection

brought the Company £5,786, but by 1942, the number of people using the station had been reduced to 13,758, and the income from these was just £298. With alternative facilities being available by road, it was clearly not worth keeping Victoria Park open, and all those present agreed it should close. Therefore, it ceased to function from 8th November 1943, and the waiting rooms on the City-bound Poplar platform handed over as a meeting place for the local Home Guard.

The former booking office of the original station survived until 1958, having been converted into a pair of houses, latterly known as 339 and 339A Wick Road, but by then piecemeal demolition had done away with much of the second establishment.

It survived fairly intact into the postwar era, but by 1950 the footbridge had gone, and probably the Riseholme Street entrance as well. Part of the main building facing onto Cadogan Square became a private house, but the station accommodation at track level became derelict. Bit by bit the station disappeared, until by the 1965, all that remained was the main building itself, and a couple of mounds where the platforms used to be. Even as late as this it was still possible to read the old name on one of its blackened windows, but little else of interest survived.

The end came in 1970, when everything was swept away to facilitate the construction of a new road, and today there are no indications to its former existence. For some time after it was demolished, the park entrance on the opposite side of Cadogan Terrace displayed the name 'Station Gate', but this has now been altered to 'Cadogan Gate'.

The signal box which formerly stood on the north side was replaced early in 1961 by a new one between the two diverging sets of lines, but this ceased to be used after the tracks to Poplar fell into disuse, and having stood derelict for a number of years, was largely demolished in the early 1990s. By the end of 1994, only its bottom section remained.

VICTORIA PARK - OLD FORD

South-east of Victoria Park, the line to Poplar was latterly used for occasional freights only, and its tracks became rusty and overgrown. By the late 1970s it had been reduced to a single line, and apart from the odd special working, the route had fallen into almost total disuse. However, within a few years a decision was made to incorporate part of it into the new Docklands Light Railway, and plans were being drawn up to shape its possible future. In connection with this, a two-car diesel unit ran up and down the line for about five hours on 9th February 1984 to assess the amount of noise caused by trains running under a high-rise estate which had been erected over the cutting south of Bow station. In fact this turned out to be the last time the route was used by BR, as three months later, on Sunday 5th May, the junction points at Victoria Park were removed, and engineers began lifting the tracks.

The section between here and Bow is now bereft of track, although the remainder of the formation through to Poplar has been taken over by the DLR.

Close to the bridge which carries the erstwhile line over the Hertford Union Canal stands the former 'Mitford Castle' public house, where the dying Mr. Briggs was carried on that fateful night in 1864. It's undergone a confusing change of identity, and is now called 'The Top O' The Mornin', but at least it bears a commemorative plaque outside which tells how it gained its little niche in history.

From Victoria Park Junction, the route continued southward, and crossed both Wick Lane and the Northern Outfall Sewer before passing beneath Old Ford Road, and reaching the site of the next station.

OLD FORD

Old Ford was opened on 1st July 1867, and had a street level building on the south side of the road. With its arched doorway centred between two groups of matching windows it looked the epitome of symmetry, but because of its siting, one end was wider than the other, and therefore the legend set in cement on the west elevation read 'North London Railway', whilst that on the east stated 'N. London Railway'. This and the track level buildings were constructed largely of

Above : The street level building at Old Ford, viewed from the west end, showing the legend *'North London Railway'* in full. Inside, the wooden booking office was situated to the left of the doorway, backing onto the frontage.

Below : View from the opposite end, with the company's title abbreviated to *'N. London Railway'*. Both photographs were taken in the autumn of 1966, about a year before the building was demolished.

Both : J.E. Connor

Above : Old Ford, looking towards Broad Street on 22nd February 1950.
Trains had ceased to call almost six years previously, but the station was still more or less intact. The supports which once held an LMS 'hawkseye' nameboard can be seen on the left.
Author's Collection

Below : Old Ford, again towards Broad Street, but this time seen in January 1966, after the platform buildings had been removed, and the platforms themselves partially demolished.
J.E. Connor

yellow stock bricks, and the platforms were reached by two covered stairways which led down from the booking office.

Some time in the 1930s, Old Ford was equipped with LMSR 'hawkseye' style nameboards, and is believed to be the only station on the Poplar branch so treated. These incorporated black lettering set against a golden yellow target shape, reminiscent of the style then used by the Southern Railway, and were very distinctive.

After nearly twenty years of disuse, the platforms and associate buildings were demolished in 1963, leaving just the booking hall which remained for a little longer before it was finally swept away in 1967. Around this time, the signal box, which stood at the south end of the City-bound platform fell into disuse, and subsequently disappeared. Nearby road alterations necessitated the replacement of the bridge over the line by a flimsy structure for pedestrians only, and latterly, the only remnants of the station itself were broken fragments of platform at its northern end.

Behind the Poplar-bound platform, and stretching virtually all the way to Tredegar Road, lay Old Ford Goods Depot, which was opened by the North London in 1868, but transferred to the LNWR two years later. It was subsequently enlarged during 1872 and 1879, and finally closed on 6th November 1967. After closure, part of it was used as a scrapyard, and a few of the buildings lasted into the 1980s. These have now gone however, and at the time of writing the site is being redeveloped.

DISASTER AT OLD FORD

The bridge which carries Tredegar Road over the former railway was the scene of a fatal collision which occurred on the night of Saturday 28th January 1882.

That evening, a train comprising fifty empty coal wagons and two brake vans left Poplar at 22.05, and slowly made its way along the branch on its journey to Brent Sidings on the Midland Railway. As it approached Old Ford, a defective drawbar beneath a truck owned by the Nuneaton firm of J.N.C. Harrison snapped in two, and the trailing section embedded itself in a sleeper, causing the rear seventeen vehicles to break away from the main part of the train. The force with which this happened was also sufficient to derail the Harrison's wagon, together with the three others which were following it, and threw them across the track fouling both sets of lines.

At around this time, the 21.50 passenger train from Broad Street had just left Old Ford station, and was beginning to gather speed on the slightly falling gradient. It was headed by 4-4-0T No.8, working bunker first, and was made up of ten coaches and two vans. Running under clear signals, it passed the goods train on the other track, but its fireman noticed that it only comprised of coal wagons, and had apparently lost its brake vans. He yelled across to his mate to warn him of the possible danger, but it was too late, and before the driver could apply his brake, the locomotive hit the wagons, and left the rails. It reeled from the track, dragging with it the leading van and a Third Class coach, and the whole lot ploughed itself into the solid brick abutment of the bridge.

The sound of the impact was heard at both Old Ford and Bow stations, and emergency measures were immediately put into hand. In the meantime however, the driver of the coal train was oblivious of what had happened, and it wasn't until he was stopped by the signalman at Victoria Park that he realised that something was wrong.

Within a short while, railway staff, aided by some local people and a group of policemen began the work of extricating the dead and injured, and three doctors were on hand to administer the necessary medical attention. All of the fatalities occurred in the Third Class coach, and amongst these victims were a young mother and her infant daughter. Apart from these, three other passengers lost their lives, and five received minor injuries.

A three-hundred strong team which comprised the breakdown gang, aided by an army of labourers, worked all night to clear the line, and by eight o'clock the following morning, both tracks were again operational. Amongst the men who were active in the rescue and clearing-up operations were the Company's General Manager, Mr. G. Bolland Newton, and the Locomotive

Superintendent, Mr. John Park.

Locomotive No.8 was towed into Bow Works for repair, and was soon returned to traffic. Quite surprisingly its damage was comparatively light, and the cost of putting it back into service was estimated at just £50.

South of the Tredegar Road bridge, the line continued southwards, and passed under the GER main line, and the Blackwall Extension Railway, before reaching the station at Bow.

The street level building at Bow in the early 1900s, with the Bow & Bromley Institute on the first floor, and Rowland Plumbe's Match Tax Testimonial Fountain fronting the forecourt. The dome-shaped construction on the west end of the building, just visible to the left accomodated the Institute's organ, used during musical recitals.

Commercial postcard : J.E. Connor Collection

BOW

Bow was one of the earliest NLR stations, but the original structure of 1850 was tiny when compared to the massive pile which was erected when it was extensively rebuilt under the direction of E. H. Horne between 1869 and 1870. The new premises were extremely impressive, and cost the Company the sum of £25,000.

Whilst the work was being carried out, a temporary station entrance was opened in Avenue Road (now Kitcat Terrace), but this was closed when the permanent building was completed on 26th March 1870. Following this, on 2nd April, *'The East London Observer'* gave this report on the new structure: *"Above the booking offices, waiting and refreshment rooms is a handsome hall stretching the whole length and breadth of the station 100 feet in length, 40 feet in width and 45 feet in height...a finer hall does not exist in the East End of London".*

The hall to which the writer refers was an integral part of the building, known as 'The Bow & Bromley Institute'. It was intended as a cultural centre, and was used for various activities including lectures and classical concerts. It was opened to the public along with the new station, and enthusiastically supported by the NLR, who encouraged its employees to take advantage of the facilities. The establishment owed its origins to two groups which had been active in the area, namely The Bromley Literary Association and the Bow Working Mens Institute. Although its organisation was nothing to do with the railway, the Company fully approved, and therefore only charged them a low rental. There was an extensive library, and from 1874, an organ as well. This had cost the Institute £800, and was paid for by patrons as a result of a regular appeal. It was made by Messrs. Brindley and Foster of Sheffield, and housed at the west end of the building.

To complete the scene of grandeur, the architect, Rowland Plumbe, a friend of Edwin Horne, erected the Match Tax Testimonial Fountain at the front of the station forecourt in 1872. This was again financed by public subscription, and commemorated the part played by the staff of the nearby Bryant & May company in securing the abandonment of a proposed tax on matches. It was an elaborate gothic styled monument, somewhat reminiscent of an Eleanor Cross, and it included a symbolic figure of justice, seated beneath an ornamental canopy.

At track level, the station consisted of four platform faces, and at one time boasted services onto the Great Eastern and London, Tilbury & Southend Railways, as well as destinations on the NLR.

The GER started working into Bow on 1st January 1869, when they took over the running of a shuttle to and from Fenchurch Street. This had previously been operated by the North London, and maintained a link which had existed since the line first opened in 1850. These trains used the west side of the station, and shared platforms with services to Broad Street and Poplar. However, as the years progressed their usage declined, and the Great Eastern decided to withdraw them. Rather than continue their operation, it was deemed more economical to re-site the existing Bow Road station on the Fenchurch Street - Stratford line, and provide it with a covered footway, giving direct access to the north end of the platforms at Bow. This was opened,

LTSR 4-4-2T No.31 'St. Pancras' awaits departure from Bow with the 7.28am Southend - Chalk Farm through train on 25th June 1912. The footbridge in the foreground led to the passageway linking Bow North London to Bow Road on the Great Eastern.

LCGB Ken Nunn Collection

along with the new GE premises on 4th April 1892, and the shuttle was discontinued.

Adjoining this narrow passageway was a claustrophobic little office, where passengers without through tickets could re-book before continuing their journey. As with the similar facility already described at Hackney, both NLR and GER tickets were available for issue. Those for the North London showed the station of origin as *'Bow No.2'*, whilst those for the Great Eastern displayed *'Bow Road (EO)'*; the initials standing for *'Exchange Office'*.

The platforms on the east side accommodated services which worked over a connecting spur linking the North London with the LTSR. This was first used on Whit Monday, 17th May 1869 for excursion traffic, and opened for ordinary trains the following day. Initially these ran between Chalk Farm and Plaistow, but were cut back to Bow after 30th September 1871. The service continued like this for many years, although for a brief spell between June 1877 and January 1878, it was again extended to Chalk Farm.

In addition to local trains, the Bow - Bromley spur was also used by longer-distance workings, particularly during the summer. Until 1886, through carriages were operated from Chalk Farm to either Tilbury or Thames Haven, where connections could be made with sailings to Margate. These were hauled as far as Plaistow by a North London engine, and then coupled to an LTSR train to continue their journey. At the same time through services ran to Southend, and these were hauled throughout by NLR motive power. All these workings ceased after the railways began to use continuous brakes, and the type used by the North London was seemingly not compatible with that on the LTSR.

In 1907, the LTSR reintroduced through trains between Chalk Farm and Southend, and operated them with their own locomotives. These proved popular, and ran throughout the summer months until the advent of war in 1914.

Another early wartime casualty was the Bow - Plaistow shuttle service. These trains had been fairly lightly loaded for some time, and were eventually withdrawn from 1st January 1915. A further cut directly attributable to the war was the closure of the footway linking the station with Bow Road on the GE. This was abandoned at the beginning of 1917, and never re-opened.

The Bow & Bromley Institute, which had become a branch of the East London Technical College in 1897, finally closed in 1911, and the hall leased to the Salvation Army. Many of the 6,000 books are believed to have been transferred to public libraries in Stepney and Poplar, and the organ was sold in 1913 to an unspecified "Popular West End place of worship." In 1933, the Salvation Army moved out and made way for a snooker club known as *'The Embassy Billiard Hall'*.

From 1st January 1923 until 27th April 1935, the LMSR ran a commuter service linking Broad Street with places on the former London Tilbury & Southend, by way of the Bow - Bromley spur. In an article published in the August 1946 edition of the magazine *'Railways'*, the writer, James F. Vickery recalls travelling on the first of these, having joined the train at Leigh-on-Sea. It consisted of eight six-wheel coaches, and was hauled by ex-LTSR 4-4-2T No.2162, which had originally carried the name *'Bow Road'*. It left Leigh at 08.44, then called all stations to Barking except Pitsea and East Horndon, then ran fast to Broad Street. It arrived in the City at 09.59, five minutes late, having suffered signal checks en-route.

On the foggy morning of 1st April 1937, Bow station was the scene of an end-on collision, which although resulting in no fatalities, was potentially nasty.

It happened as the peak period was reaching its height, and involved the 07.17 and 07.28 trains to Broad Street.

As was to be expected in such weather conditions, the trains were running late, and the 07.17 was still waiting to leave at 07.30. Its driver had begun to release his brakes in readiness to depart, when the empty stock for the following service plunged into the rear. The impact caused the last two coaches of the stationary train to telescope each other, and fifteen people were injured.

The guard of the 07.17 was fortunately standing on the platform at the time, otherwise he would almost certainly have been killed. Nevertheless, with his head bleeding from a piece of flying glass, he grabbed a saw, and began cutting through the wrecked coach bodies to help release the people who were trapped.

After the crash there was a degree of public concern over the use of wood for the bodies of passenger stock, and in answer to this, an LMS spokesman was quoted in a national daily as saying that only 1.8% of his company's existing vehicles had been built in this manner, and these were only used on suburban lines. As it was suburban passengers who were concerned for their safety, his words of reassurance were perhaps a little pointless.

The cause of the Bow accident was attributed to an error on behalf of the signalman at Devons Road, who had been distracted by a telephone call regarding the duties of a local fog-man, and therefore inadvertently allowed two trains in section at the same time.

When closure came in 1944, Bow had already become a sad looking place, as in common with so many stations, it had suffered the ravages of war. Admittedly, the buildings remained large-ly intact, but by that time everything had taken on a run-down appearance.

The 'News Chronicle' for 31st March 1948 described the condition of the station nearly four years after closure: "Its clock has stopped at 9.26. The nameboards have been taken down, and the win-dows of its waiting rooms are grimy and broken. Even the Tyburn Sports Club which once made a wait-ing room its headquarters have gone..."

The neighbouring ex-GER station was the next to go, being closed permanently from 7th November 1949, when the Fenchurch Street - Stratford trains were withdrawn. Although this line had been used by passenger traffic throughout the war years, Bow Road station itself had not, having been out of commission for two lengthy periods between 1941 and 1947.

The old Bow & Bromley Institute was used for billiards, and found itself leased out as a dance hall, first known as 'The Bow Palais', and latterly 'The Emerald Ballroom'. In this guise it was badly damaged by fire in 1956, resulting in the building's partial demolition. Prior to this, the Bryant & May Match Tax Testimonial Fountain was demolished in 1953, leaving just a small plaque adjacent to Poplar Town Hall to acknowledge where it once stood. The lower part of the station building, including the old booking office, was retained by British Railways, and used as a parcels depot, until the early part of 1965.

Now everything was abandoned. A certain amount of demolition had already been carried out at track level, and the once busy station presented a very sorry sight indeed. The footbridge at the north end, which linked to the interchange footway had gone by 1950, as had the canopy on the down Bromley platform. The remainder continued to stand until 1963, although by this time more of the awnings had been removed, and the place was looking very derelict. By 1966, all that remained was the ruins of the booking hall, together with a few other buildings on the London-bound Poplar line platform, and the bricked-off footway. These structures managed to linger on for a little longer, but after becoming extremely shabby, were largely obliterated in November 1975.

After the track was lifted, the station area became hidden beneath a jungle of foliage, and it was virtually impossible to see any of the scanty remains which had survived.

However, in 1985, work commenced on the Poplar - Stratford section of the Docklands Light Railway, and the site was cleared to facilitate the construction of a new rising embankment. This was to take the trains from the old North London formation, and carry them up to the level of the Great Eastern line.

For a while, the derelict interchange footway, which in later days had been used as a small biscuit factory, remained more or less intact, but this was partly demolished in the early 1990s, and little has been left standing.

At the time of writing, the trackbed between Bow and Victoria Park remains derelict, although a section of it has been landscaped and converted into a walkway. An old water tower continues to stand on the east side of the cutting, and appears to be in reasonable condi-tion. This adjoins the site of Bow goods depot, which was opened by the LNWR on 20th March 1893, and functioned until 1940. The main part of the depot was situated to the west of the for-mation, although sidings existed on both sides of the line.

A pathetic fragment of wall from the once impressive passenger station frontage survives, and until recently provided the backdrop for a car dealer who traded on the former forecourt.

Above : Bow station, looking towards Poplar on 22nd February 1950.

Below : Bow, seen on the same occasion, but from the opposite direction, In the distance, an ex-LMS *'Jinty'* heads towards Stratford with a freight train, having just passed through the then recently closed station at Bow Road on the former Great Eastern.

Both : Author's Collection

Above : The Bromley line platforms at Bow, looking towards Dalston Junction
on 22nd February 1950.

Below : A general view of Bow from the south, taken on the same date.
The building on the right, behind Bow Junction signal box formed the entrance
to the North London Railway locomotive, carriage and wagon works.

Both : Author's Collection

Above : The upper storey of Bow station, which formerly housed the Bow & Bromley Institute, during the early stages of demolition in January 1957.

B. P. Pask

Below : The remains of Bow station frontage, as it appeared during the mid-1960s. The building had been used as a parcels depot, but closed in1965.

J.E. Connor

In the early 1990s, the 'Bow Neighbourhood' council erected a blue plaque at the west end of this commemorating the station, and stating that it opened in 1870. Although this is technically true when referring to the later building, the station itself was first brought into use in 1850, and therefore the date shown is inaccurate.

Beyond the road bridge, the connecting line from the North London to Fenchurch Street branched off sharply to the right, and climbed on a gradient of 1 in 99 until it reached the level of the Blackwall Extension viaduct at Gas Factory Junction. After withdrawal of the regular passenger trains in 1892, it was used for freight, but finally closed from 29th December 1967, and subsequently lifted. The last ever passenger train to travel over it was an enthusiasts' special, organised by The Railway Correspondence & Travel Society, which ran on Saturday 21st October 1967. Sections of the trackbed still remain, but are very overgrown.

The present DLR Bow Church station, opened to the public on 31st August 1987, stands immediately beyond the bridge carrying the main road, and its southbound platform occupies the approximate site of Bow Junction signal box, which once controlled movements over the line up to Fenchurch Street.

BOW WORKS

In the cramped area between the diverging tracks at the junction once stood the original buildings of Bow Locomotive Works, which were opened in 1863. These consisted of a long two-road erecting shop, together with facilities for the smiths and boiler makers, and it was here that the Company built and serviced many of its engines.

On the opposite side of the Poplar line was situated the locomotive running shed, although this was later transferred to Devons Road when its site was required for a works extension in 1882.

Bow Works was founded by the Company's Locomotive Engineer, William Adams, and remained in use for nearly a century.

Adams was a Londoner, who spent his formative years growing-up in the East End. He was born at Limehouse in 1823, and was the son of the resident engineer of the East & West India Docks Company. He began his working life as an apprentice with a local firm of engineers and millwrights, and was later employed by the Sardinian Navy. Whilst abroad he married, then returned to England to take up his post with the NLR in 1853. He stayed with the Company until 1873, when he left to work for the GER at Stratford. After a stay of five years he again moved on, and took up the position of Locomotive Superintendent of the LSWR at Nine Elms.

The works buildings of 1882 were larger than their predecessors, and stood between the Poplar line and the spur to the LTSR. They were entered through an obscure little doorway opposite Bow station, and from here a flight of steps led down to an area which was known as 'Bow Palace Yard'. There was also a lineside catwalk which originated from the Poplar-bound platform, but this was installed solely for the convenience of the staff, and was never intended as an official entrance.

After the 1882 alterations, the whole works and depot complex at Bow covered an area of around thirty-three acres, and stretched for about three-quarters of a mile alongside the running lines.

There was a narrow alleyway connecting Campbell Road with Devons Road, which was carried on a bridge over the top of the works, and adjoined the end wall of the new erecting shop. This alley commenced opposite the east end of Archibald Street, and was segregated from the railway by high brick walls. South of here was positioned the machine and carriage shops, whilst further on still could be found the building which housed the locomotive stores.

When the LNWR took control early in 1909, they phased out the original 1863 section, which was eventually closed and demolished. Prior to this, the works employed around 750 men in its various departments, but this number dwindled after the reorganisation, and many of the former employees found themselves without a job. Then as now, unemployment brought cruel hardship, and the majority of displaced workers received only two, or at the best, three weeks' money as redundancy pay. Most of them applied for assistance from the Relieving Officer

Above : The Bow - Gas Factory Junction spur, which enabled the earliest North London passenger services to reach Fenchurch Street, seen here on 15th October 1962. It ceased to be served by regular passenger trains in 1892, but was retained for freight traffic until the late 1960s. A section of Bow Works can be seen on the right.

Below : The now obliterated earthworks of the Bow NL - Bromley LTS spur, taken from the overbridge between Campbell Road and Priscilla Road on 15th October 1962. The track had been lifted in 1959. Bow Works is to the right of the formation.

Both J.S. Phillips

appointed by the Poplar Board of Guardians, but he could offer them little, and invariably the men went without, and their families had to scrape a living the best way they could.

Despite this partial closure however, Bow Works continued to function, and actually became busier in early LMS days. The reason for this being that the new company had inherited two loco works very close to each other, and they really needed only one. The other establishment was that of the former LTSR at Plaistow, which they believed to be of less value to them than the one at Bow. Therefore, in the summer of 1925, this was abandoned, and its staff and machinery transferred to the North London premises, where they continued to maintain both native engines, and those from the Tilbury line.

In this manner the works survived well into the British Railways era, and it continued to overhaul locomotives until the late 1950s. After this, the Carriage and Wagon Department lingered on for a little longer, but eventually the premises fell into complete disuse, and the majority of the empty buildings were finally demolished around 1966.

Seven years previously, the spur which ran behind them connecting the North London with the LTSR at Bromley was deemed to be of no further use, and therefore lifted.

Much of the works site is now occupied by a high-rise development which was erected in the 1970s, and the tracks beneath are encased in a concrete cut and cover tunnel.

Beyond this, the route passes beneath the LTS line, just west of Bromley-by-Bow station. The sole surviving section of the works complex, namely the former carriage shop, stood on the east side of the formation, and actually lasted long enough to witness the passage of DLR trains. It was finally demolished in the late 1980s however, and the site has been redeveloped.

DEVONS ROAD DLR

Immediately south of Devons Road can be found the platforms of the DLR station which carries that name, and adjoining this is a famous public house, called 'The Widow's Son'. According to legend, a widow lived in a cottage on the site, and had a habit of putting aside a hot cross bun for her son when he came home on leave from the Navy every Easter. One year however, he failed to return, but she continued hanging up buns in the kitchen until she died, hoping that one day he would appear. The pub has continued this tradition for over 170 years, and each year a new bun is added to those already there. Although some are very black and shrivelled, other remain in remarkably good condition, and are presumably preserved by their high yeast content.

DEVONS ROAD MOTIVE POWER DEPOT

Devons Road running sheds were situated to the east of the line, and stretched southwards as far as the Limehouse Cut. They were opened in 1882 to replace the earlier establishment near Bow station, and in steam days they provided motive power for the majority of trains out of Broad Street. The entrance was situated at the south end of Brickfield Road, opposite 'The Beehive' public house, and the depot was built on land which had been acquired by the NLR some years earlier. On another part of this site, the Company established rows of terraced houses for its employees, and these stood in Devas Street, Marner Street and Empson Street.

The depot was erected under the instruction of the Locomotive Superintendent, Mr. John Park, and comprised two sheds, referred to as 'No.1' and 'No.2', which backed onto the north bank of the canal. These each contained ten roads, and their general styling with northlight roofs clearly showed a degree of LNWR influence. 'No.1' shed was closest to the running lines, and was provided with an adjoining coal stage, whilst watering facilities were available at the rear of 'No.2'. Various modifications were carried out in the mid-Thirties, including the demolition of 'No.2' shed, which was latterly used for storing dead engines, and the construction of a new concrete mechanical coaling plant.

From 1st March 1926, Devons Road received the LMS shed code '11', which had previously denoted Warwick. However, during the summer of 1934, it was transferrred to the Midland Division, together with its allocation of 73 locomotives, and in January 1935 it received the number 13B, which placed it in the same group as sheds on the former LTSR.

The depot survived the war, but the surrounding area was badly pasted by enemy action.

During the 1940s, a new 'louvre' roof was added to the surviving shed, but no other alterations were carried out, until 1957, when it was announced that Devons Road would become Britain's first all diesel depot.

As previously mentioned, the depot had been grouped with sheds on the former LTSR, but when that line was transferred to the Eastern Region in 1949, Devons Road was renumbered 1D, therefore bringing it under the same banner as ex-LNW London area sheds such as Willesden (1A) and Camden (1B).

At the time of its closure to steam it had an allocation of forty-one locomotives, and the last of these, 'Jinty' 0-6-0T No.47517 departed on 25th August 1958. After this, the shed became home to thirty-three diesels, although withdrawn steam engines were occasionally transferred there for storage until 1964. Amongst these were rebuilt 'Patriot' 4-6-0, No.45529 'Stephenson', rebuilt 'Jubilee' 4-6-0, No.45735 'Comet', and the sole surviving ex-GE B12, No.61572. The last mentioned of these was later acquired for preservation, and has recently been restored to working order for use on the North Norfolk Railway at Sheringham.

With BR's modernisation plan in full swing, Devons Road was soon eclipsed by larger, better equipped diesel depots, and its locos were gradually reallocated elsewhere. Renumbered 1J in its final days, it was closed from 10th February 1964, and the remaining engines transferred to Stratford. It stood derelict for a number of years but was eventually demolished, and its site cleared for redevelopment.

DEVONS ROAD GOODS DEPOT

On the opposite side of the Poplar branch was Devons Road Goods & Coal Depot, which was opened by the LNWR purely for coal traffic in July 1874, and enlarged to handle additional freight in February 1891. Late on the night of Saturday 23rd September 1916, it became the target of a Zeppelin raid, when four bombs struck the line south of Bow station, and severed the connection into the yard. Damage to the trackwork was severe, and seven passenger coaches in the nearby carriage sidings were damaged beyond repair. Four members of staff were injured, but fortunately there were no fatalities. The civil engineers worked throughout the Sunday, and despite having to contend with obstacles such as a 15ft. wide by 8ft. deep bomb crater, traffic was restored by Monday morning.

In common with similar facilities elsewhere in the area, Devons Road Goods eventually succumbed to the road competition, and was closed from 2nd November 1964.

Adjoining the canal could be found the sidings serving the Lea Cut Coal Wharf. This had been opened as early as 1851, and had its name expanded to 'Lea & Limehouse Cut' at the turn of the century. It survived a little longer than Devons Road, but eventually closed around 1970.

SOUTH BROMLEY

South of the Limehouse Cut, the route passes the impressive red-brick factory built in 1899 by the well-known pet food manufacturers, Spratts, and now converted into flats and workshops.

Alongside is the site of South Bromley, the last station constructed by the NLR on the Poplar line, and the only one to consist of a single island platform.

It was opened on 1st September 1884, and was entered through an inconspicuous doorway at the east end of Rifle Street, adjoining the premises of 'The Far Famed Cake Company'. From here, a flight of stairs led up to the brick booking office above the tracks, and a further stairway provided access to the platform. The site was very cramped, and clearly showed that the station was added as an afterthought.

In its early days it saw considerable passenger traffic, but was never as busy as other stations on the line. Because of its close proximity to Devons Road, the last train of the day would terminate there, and therefore crews on this working had to ensure their engine was equipped with a South Bromley destination board.

The station was the scene of a mysterious fire in May 1913, which was locally rumoured to have been started by suffragettes. The blaze originated in a porters room on the platform in the small hours of a Friday morning, and by the time the Fire Brigade arrived, it had got a strong

An extremely rare view of the little photographed station at South Bromley, looking towards Poplar in the late 1930s. The original print appears to have been taken on a box camera, and is the only one known to the author which shows the platform buildings

David Hanson Collection

hold, and had spread to an adjacent lamp room. Ninety firemen, working with four motor pumps and other appliances fought the inferno for over two hours, but despite their efforts, the flames took their toll, leaving the booking office, and wooden flooring seriously damaged. At first it was thought that the bridge over the line had become too dangerous for public use, but thanks to some emergency carpentry, it was strengthened in time for the start of the morning's service, and the charred station opened for traffic as normal.

During the Second World War the booking office was badly damaged by bombing, and tickets were latterly issued from the platform waiting room. To reach this, passengers had to cross the City bound line, and were led across the track by a flagman.

After closure in 1944, it wasn't long before demolition of the ruined buildings was put in hand, and by the summer of 1948 they had virtually disappeared. All that survived was the lower part of the booking office bridge, the platform itself, and a few truncated lamp posts. The signal box, which stood at the north end of the station was still in use and therefore retained.

In time, relics of the former station became less and less, until by the mid-1960s the only remnant was an overgrown mound which indicated the site of the platform. This lasted until 1985, when it was removed during the construction of the DLR, and South Bromley has now completely vanished. All that can be seen today are chipped cement plaques on a wall to the west of the line which display the name of 'The Far Famed Cake Company', but despite their apparent permanence, the firm which they advertise is long closed, and has faded into history.

SOUTH BROMLEY - POPLAR

Beyond South Bromley, the line passes slightly east of that showpiece of 1951, The Lansbury Development. This was named after George Lansbury, the justifiably famous Labour MP, and was intended to point the way towards better working class housing in the hopeful years which followed the Second World War. It was designed and presented as an extension of the

Festival of Britain which was then being held on the South Bank near Waterloo station, and when new, it added a touch of cheer to the gloomy war-damaged skyline. Fortunately it survives, although the attractive clocktower, from which one could command a superb vista, both of the adjacent Chrisp Street market, and Poplar in general, has now been locked up to prevent vandalism.

The street level building at Poplar East India Road, in the first decade of the twentieth century. The present DLR All Saints station now occupies most of the site, although a tiny fragment of the original frontage still remains.

Commercial postcard : Michael Cox Collection

POPLAR, EAST INDIA ROAD

Once under the East India Dock Road bridge, the line reaches the DLR platforms of All Saints, which were opened in 1987 on the site of the former North London Poplar station.

Opened on 1st August 1866, Poplar was for many years the terminus for passenger trains from Broad Street. It was always known as 'Poplar East India Road', and for the majority of its existence was served by four trains an hour, both to and from the City.

In appearance it was similar to Old Ford, already described, with a neat, single-storey booking hall on the south side of the main road, and two stairways leading down to the platforms. At track level, the lines continued through the station until reaching the bridge carrying Poplar High Street, where they diverged. One of the routes headed south-west towards the goods yard at Harrow Lane, whilst the other continued south-east towards Blackwall.

This second curve was first brought into use in 1852, but was originally intended for goods traffic only. After the NLR introduced a passenger service to Poplar, this was relaid, and through trains from Broad Street to Blackwall commenced running on 1st September 1870. After leaving NL metals these trains ran non-stop to Blackwall, and therefore never called at the L&B Poplar station in Brunswick Street. At first these workings were presumably popular, and the North London began issuing tickets to Woolwich and Gravesend, which were valid on connecting steamers from Blackwall. In time however, patronage dropped, and the trains were cut back to Poplar East India Road from 1st July 1890. This decision was obviously intended to be final, as the junction between the two companies was severed the following month.

The station was once served by two signal boxes; one at the north end called East India Dock Road, and one to the south known as High Street. Both of these were abolished from 9th September 1888, and replaced by a new cabin named Poplar Central.

'BRITAIN'S MOST BOMBED STATION'

Poplar East India Road suffered badly during the Second World War, and reputedly became Britain's most bombed passenger station. On various occasions, the lines around it were damaged, and every time they were patched up again. In May 1941, Poplar Central signal box, which stood to the south of the platforms, was almost totally destroyed when a land-mine exploded on top of one of the nearby railway retaining walls. However, in less than two weeks, and after a great deal of work in far from ideal conditions, it was rebuilt, virtually like for like, and put back into commission.

Services between Dalston Junction and Poplar were regularly subject to interruption during the war years, and they were finally suspended from 15th May 1944. The following month, the first flying bomb to land on LMS property exploded on the west side of the cutting, behind the platform, and damaged the station beyond repair. In March 1947, the demolition men moved in and tore down what was left of the ruined buildings. It seems likely that South Bromley was similarly dealt with at the same time.

All that remained at Poplar were the two platforms, and the lower part of the booking hall. These survived virtually unchanged until they were removed in 1985 to provide a site for the new DLR station. Today there are virtually no reminders of the old building, except an obscure fragment of frontage which is just about recognisable at street level.

Ex-North Staffordshire Railway 2-4-0T No.1451, in fully lined LMS crimson lake livery brings the empty stock for a Broad Street service into Poplar on a very murky 16th January 1927. Together with Nos.1442, 1446, 1447, and 1450 of the same class, 1451 had been transferred to Devons Road for working North London services, but the engines lacked the necessary power, and were soon returned to their native district.

No.1451 was first outshopped from Stoke in June 1895, rebuilt with larger boiler and improved cab in 1904, and finally withdrawn for scrapping in February 1928.

H.C. Casserley

HARROW LANE YARD

Beyond All Saints, the Docklands Light Railway trains head southwards, then take a sharp curve before reaching their next station which is called Poplar. En-route, they pass a large building to the west of the line, which at first glance could be mistaken as part of a former NLR passenger station. In fact it was the Goods Superintendent's Office for the nearby Harrow Lane yard. Engineers working here in 1985 discovered a row of square holes near its base, and deduced that it once had a wooden platform. Around this time the old roofing slates were replaced, and cleaning has transformed its sooty brickwork back to its original colouring.

Harrow Lane goods yard comprised numerous sidings, and adjoined the north side of the London & Blackwall line. It was opened in 1866, and provided with a physical connection to the L&B in 1873. It survived longer than other yards in the area, but had fallen into disuse by the early 1980s. After closure the site was cleared, and part of it is now occupied by the DLR Operations & Maintenance Centre.

POPLAR DOCKS

South of Poplar, tracks climbed on gradients of 1 in 29 and 1 in 34, and crossed the London & Blackwall by means of bridges. These lines served the various goods and coal depots around the docks, and were first brought into use on 1st January 1852.

The North London's own establishment opened for coal traffic on 20th October 1851, and for general freight on 1st January 1852. This was followed on 12th March, the following year, by the LNWR who opened a depot near Prestons Road.

Other companies soon approached the NLR with a view to constructing goods depots in the area, and the first of these was the Great Northern. The North London responded favourably and built a warehouse with accompanying sidings specifically for their use in 1868. This sufficed for a while, but extra traffic demanded larger premises, and within ten years, the GNR found it necessary to expand. Their enlarged depot opened on 1st September 1878, which was five months to the day after yet another company, the Great Western, had opened a goods station at Poplar Dock, also served by the NLR.

Because of the steep gradients involved, the route between Poplar station and the docks proved difficult to work, and therefore the track layout was later modified. In 1875 a loop line was added which commenced in Harrow Lane Yard, and climbed to join the original bridges over the London & Blackwall. Once this was completed the majority of dock trains were routed via Harrow Lane, where they reversed and then travelled over this new connection.

There were three signal boxes in the immediate area, the first of these was called Blackwall Bridge, and was positioned near the spot where the North London crossed over the L&B. The others were at Loop Line Junction, and Harrow Lane, but the latter was closed in March 1909, when its duties were transferred to Blackwall Bridge.

On the piece of land between the south-eastern curve from Poplar station, and the London & Blackwall line stood the North London's hydraulic power station, which once supplied the energy to drive the various cranes and other machinery in the area. This consisted of four contiguous buildings, and was constructed largely of yellow stock bricks. Starting at the north end, there was a two storey building with a flat roof, used as a fitter's shop and stores, and this was followed by the boilerhouse, which until the mid-1930s boasted a tall chimney. Immediately to the south stood the accumulator tower, and next door to this was the engine house.

In its heyday, the railway system around Poplar Dock was a fascinating, bustling network, but enemy action during the Second World War, and the later effects of road competition eventually killed it all off.

The first big raid of the Blitz, 7th September 1940, known locally as 'Black Saturday', left much of the area devastated, and the large GWR Poplar Goods Station virtually destroyed. After a night of airborne holocaust suffered by the people of east London, The Ministry of Home Security glibly stated that the attack was "Serious but not crippling". Of course, this was just the beginning, and far worse was to come. In the period of a month, between 7th October and 6th November 1940, the Poplar district was hit by 102 high explosive bombs, 4 oil bombs, and 5 groups of incendiaries. With such relentless evil dropping from the skies, it's no wonder that by the time the war ended, a great deal of the East End had been reduced to ruins.

The GWR establishment was never repaired, but the various other depots around Poplar continued to function into the postwar era. By the 1960s however traffic was on the decline, and parts of the system began to fall into disuse. After the abandonment of the former L&B east of Millwall Junction, the remaining track was lifted, and the opportunity was taken to realign the North London approach to the docks. The old high level route was closed, and replaced by a more direct line which cut across the former Blackwall formation. This was brought into use in May 1968, and within just over a year the earlier alignment had been completely removed. Following these modifications the signal boxes at Poplar Central and Blackwall Bridge were rendered redundant, and subsequently demolished.

The amount of rail traffic into and out of the docks became less and less with more freight than ever going by road, and the rails to Poplar began to look decidedly rusty. The line was eventually singled, and became very overgrown.

The coming of the Docklands Light Railway, and the drastic redevelopment which has occurred in the area, has eradicated virtually everything of the erstwhile infrastructure of Poplar Dock, and standing on the site today, it's almost impossible to envisage the scene as it once was.

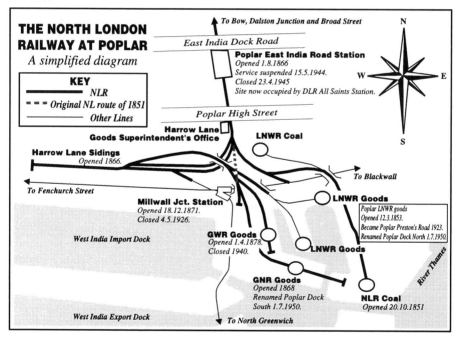

SELECT BIBLIOGRAPHY
Various publications were consulted during the production of this book,
but special mention should be made of the following:
Chronology of London's Railways : H.V. Borley (*Railway & Canal Historical Society 1982*)
London's Termini : Alan A. Jackson (*David & Charles : 2nd Edition 1985*)
Memories and Writings of A London Railwayman - A Tribute to Harold Vernon Borley (1895 - 1989)
H.V. Borley : Edited by Alan A. Jackson (*Railway & Canal Historical Society 1993.*)
North London Railway Historical Society Journal : particularly No.6 (Spring 1992) - Dunloe Street
signal box by David Hanson, and No.14 (Autumn 1994) - Broad Street station, also by David Hanson
The North London Railway : Michael Robbins (*Oakwood Press 6th Edition 1967*)